Rome &

A Study in Jewish Nationalism

By
Moses Hess

ANODOS
BOOKS

Moses Hess (1812-1875), Meyer Waxman (1887-1969).
Originally published in 1918.

Anodos Books
1c Kings Road
Whithorn
Newton Stewart
Dumfries & Galloway
DG8 8PP

Contents

Translator's Preface

It was Ruskin who divided all books into two classes: into books of the hour and books for all time. To the first belong the great majority of books; to the second, the few and chosen. To the latter belongs *Rome and Jerusalem*. It is as timely to-day as it was fifty-six years ago, when it first saw the light of day; and, in a sense, even more timely, for *Rome and Jerusalem* belongs to the very few books which are written in advance of their time.

To-day, when Zionism has grown from a mere dream in the minds of a few, to a great ideal which is the goal of a great organization, and Jewish Nationalism has become a mighty force in Jewish life, the translator feels confident that an English version of *Rome and Jerusalem,* the herald of Nationalism and trumpet of Zionism, will certainly find a welcome reception among those to whom the future of the Jewish people is a matter of deep concern. For the book bears a message to the Zionist and non-Zionist alike. To the first it supplies the philosophic basis and the depth of thought which are essential for the conception as well as the realization of his ideal. To the second it furnishes a broader view of Judaism and of the Jewish problem and its solution.

The translation has been a labor of love. My thanks are due to the Publishers, who have encouraged me to undertake the work, and especially to my friend, Dr. B. A. Elzas, who read the manuscript and offered valuable suggestions.

Meyer Waxman.

New York, April, 1918.

AMONG the many notable Jews which the nineteenth century produced, who have profoundly influenced the course of events of the world history in general, and of Jewry in particular, Moses Hess holds a prominent place. His services on behalf of the Jewish National Movement, he having been the first to supply Jewish Nationalism with a philosophic basis, undoubtedly entitle him to such a place. But his original contribution to Jewish thought, his raising of the Jewish view to the dignity of a world view, elevate him to a much higher plane. Hess, like the Prophets of old, was ahead of his times, and saw dreams and visions in the distant future. And though his own generation did not manifest a proper appreciation of his ideas, still as time passed on and the seeds which he sowed have gradually borne fruit, and the Jewish National Movement, of which he was the Prophet, became a vital force in the life of world Jewry, the writings of Hess have attracted more and more attention. It is especially interesting at the present moment, when we are in the grip of a world war, and are expecting events which may have a lasting effect on the future of Jews and Judaism, to study the words of this thinker, to whom Judaism is more than mere dogmatism and Jewish Nationalism more than a striving toward the establishment of a petty political State, but both combined, forming a mighty intellectual, spiritual, and social force in the life of humanity in general, and Jewry in particular. Yet with all his originality, Hess was, after all, a child of his time; and in his book *Rome and Jerusalem* are mirrored all the different tendencies of the age, so that in order to grasp its full importance, we must have a bird's-eye view of all the currents, political and intellectual, which swayed the general and Jewish life of that period.

The first half of the nineteenth century was a turbulent time for Germany. It was the period during which the gradual genesis of the German Empire and the birth of its Constitution took place. And, as in all periods of generation, struggle was its chief feature. The foundation for the strivings toward unity and democracy was laid by Napoleon who, through his Confederacy of the South German States, and their model Constitutional government, proved to the Germans the value of these two political boons. The youth of Germany, responding to the call to arms in the War of Liberation against Napoleon, hoped to liberate Germany not only from foreign rule, but also from petty tyranny and autocracy.

They were, however, bitterly disappointed in their hopes. The Holy Alliance, the dominating spirit of which was Metternich, strove with all the power at its disposal to obstruct these tendencies. It was to its interest to keep Germany split into small States, so as to avoid the rise of the people against their rulers. It therefore attempted to perpetuate this division by incorporating it in the Articles of the German Confederation which were forced upon Germany by Metternich. And thus the struggle began.

The strugglers were of two different types, the Conservatives or Nationalists, and the Liberals or Radicals. The Nationalists, led originally by Turnvater Jahn (mentioned frequently by Hess in his letters), the one who founded the gymnastic societies known as *Turnvereinen*, were extreme chauvinists and reactionary in their tendencies, with the exception of their demand for a constitutional government. The Liberals, influenced by the French ideals of liberty, equality, and fraternity, were mentally of a revolutionary attitude. In the thirties, there was added to the political influence of France also the social. The rise of a laboring class, as a result of the development of industry, brought in its wake a new problem, the economic. The theories which attempt to find the solution to this problem by proposing a change in the distribution of wealth, and later became known as Socialism, found many adherents in Germany. There was, of course, no hard and fast line of division between the various tendencies. All kinds of dreamers and visionaries found a hearing. Their common enemy was the autocratic government. Even later, when Socialism began to crystallize itself as a distinct class movement, it still united forces in the political struggle with the Liberals. The center of both wings, the Nationalists and the Liberals, were the Universities. It was the intellectual class, the professors, students, writers of all stamps and brands, who were the leaders in this popular struggle, and mostly on the Liberal side. The government sought to repress the movement, but the more it was repressed, the more it spread among the masses. The Liberal movement reached its height in the forties, and culminated in the Revolution of 1848. This Revolution, however, ended in a failure. It satisfied only the Nationalistic claims. It brought Germany a step nearer to unification, and introduced constitutional government, but the Radicals, who had expected a complete overthrow of Monarchy, and the Socialists, who awaited the approach of the Social Revolution, despaired of their aims, and turned to other activities. Some were exiled from Germany; among them was Hess. The trend of German life after 1848 was more of a Nationalistic type, which finally culminated in the unification of Germany in 1870.

The political struggle was only the outward expression of an inner conflict of different intellectual currents. The intellectual aspect of Germany in the last three decades of the first half of the century presented a veritable eddy of ideas, tendencies, and spiritual movements. The center of the field was held by Hegelianism. Of all the German philosophical systems, there was none which influenced the course of political and social events so profoundly as this. Hegel's great contribution to human thought is his application of the concept of evolution to life and thought. His *Dialectics* is nothing but a property of thought, in virtue of which each particular thought passes over into another. And when applied to life, it supplies a view which looks upon each particular thing as belonging together with all other things. Hegel saw in history a continual unfolding and growth, and not a mere succession of stable and fixed events.

It is this central thought of Hegelianism, which stirred young Germany to action, Hegel himself, it is true, arrived at different conclusions in his political philosophy, and saw in the Bureaucratic State the highest expression of the *Spirit,* but his younger followers drew opposite conclusions from his own philosophy. If history means growth and change, then the old State institutions handed down from Mediæval times cannot remain in their integrity, and, consequently, a demand for changes was voiced by young Germany, the followers of the great philosopher.

A second factor in the intellectual unrest of Germany at the time was the religious question. Hegel's religious philosophy, like his political, gave rise to controversies. The question arose: "Is religion compatible with philosophy or not?" This question divided the Hegelian camp into two, the right and left wings. The height of the conflict was reached with the appearance of a book by David Friedrich Strauss *The Life of Jesus,* where the central figure of Christianity is stripped of all its divine attire and relegated to the sphere of mythology. This book immediately became the center of a storm which raised many bitter controversies. On the one hand, it caused a strong defense of Christianity, and, on the other, it gave rise to more and more extreme ideas about religion. In the left camp, Christianity, and with it all religion, was vigorously attacked, and its foundations undermined.

But when the old religious ideals were being dethroned, something had to be put in its place to satisfy the craving of men for worship. It was then that Feuerbach stepped forth with his idea of Man. The salvation and elevation of Man is, according to him, to become the religious ideal. Humanity should take the place of Divinity. These ideas gave rise, in the forties, to the Humanitarian movement, with its cosmopolitan tendencies. But how really humanitarian the movement was, can be seen from the attitude of Bauer, one of the leading humanitarians, toward the emancipation of the Jews. He published, in 1842, a pamphlet about the *Judenfrage* in which he vigorously opposes Jewish emancipation, on the ground that the Jews, by adhering to their religion, excluded themselves from emancipation. The words of Hess that "pure human nature," of which the humanitarians boast, is nothing but "pure Teutonic nature," characterize the real essence of their humanitarianism.

A third element in the intellectual leaven of Germany was the rise of the demand for social justice. The growth of industry in European countries brought to the front the glaring injustice done to the exploited classes and set people thinking about Society and its institutions. The resulting theories were known as Socialism, Communism, and Anarchism. They often conflicted with each other. Some came to the conclusion that, in order to remedy the evil, a strong socialization of all human forces is necessary. Others preached extreme Individualism and the removal of all control; and still others expounded a doctrine of moderate Individualism in the form of Communism. Thus intellectual Germany formed a motley of ideas, Liberalism, Humanitarianism, Socialism and Anarchism, all mingled into a kaleidoscopic phenomenon of conceptions, where different intellectual currents crossed each other, touched each other and diverged from each other. They had, however, one thing in common, and that was the striving toward the political liberation of Germany.

In this whirlwind of ideas and tendencies, Hess lived and acted. He reacted to all of them, and these various ideas are mirrored in his book *Rome and Jerusalem*. A general survey was necessary in order to understand his main thoughts.

The unrest and the struggle going on in the general German world was strongly reflected in the Jewish world, and there accentuated by circumstances. It worked havoc in the ranks of Jewry, and brought about a disintegration of its vital forces. The movement of enlightenment, started by Mendelssohn and his group of intellectuals in the last part of the eighteenth century, which had for its aim the harmonization of Judaism with the modern rationalistic spirit, finally culminated, in the second and third decade of the nineteenth century, in a tremendous impetus for assimilation.

The brief Napoleonic reign in Germany freed the Jews from the shackles of the Mediæval ages; it removed them from the walls of the Ghettos and placed them, for a time, on an equal footing with the rest of the inhabitants. During this brief period the entire Jewish economic and educational position was changed. The petty traders and laborers among them diminished, and their place was taken by merchants and professional men, many of whom were admitted to high positions in social life and participated in German culture. After the War of Liberation, which brought but little relief to the Jews, their legal restrictions having been mostly restored, the position of these half-emancipated Jews became precarious. They refused to be forced back in the legal and social Ghetto from which they had just emerged, and, as a result, many sought refuge from their abnormal position in conversion.

There were, however, those who did not despair entirely and hoped to continue, by means of organized effort, the struggle for emancipation and at the same time to stem the tide of conversion. The result of these efforts was the Reform movement, which took shape in the thirties and which reached its climax in the following decades. To accomplish the latter aim, namely, to bring Judaism in accord with the progressive spirit of the age, these people thought that all that was necessary was to spiritualize its content, and to abolish as many ceremonies and laws as possible. As for obtaining emancipation, it was necessary, in their opinion, to abolish Jewish Nationalism and declare the Jews to be merely a religious sect, and thus refute, once for all, the accusations of the Germans of all stamps, whether reactionary or liberal, that the Jews are an alien element.

Emancipation was obtained, though not by means of Reform. It was achieved through the political and social circumstances of the revolutionary year 1848. But assimilation was not stemmed. The extreme spiritualization of Judaism of the radical reformers and the elimination of the National element, brought the new type of Judaism within dangerous approach to reformed Christianity, the line of demarcation between them becoming almost imperceptible. Many did not hesitate, therefore, to cross this line and enjoy the social advantages which the crossing afforded.

But in the innermost recesses of the Jewish soul there smoldered yet a spark, that was finally kindled into a flame, which helped to sustain Judaism in these dangerous times and to supply it with a content. This was the creation of Jewish science. Jewish science, which taught at least a part of the Jews in Germany to respect and revere their glorious past, aroused in their hearts the feeling of self-consciousness and pride in their religion and nation, and thus helped to partly stem the tide of total assimilation. It is true, that in the beginning, Jewish science was utilized by some of its greatest builders to justify the inauguration of reform in Judaism, but it soon assumed a more conservative tendency. Such men as Rappoport, Krochmal, Graetz, Frankel and Luzzato turned it into more wholesome channels, which finally conveyed strength and support to the tottering Judaism of Germany and, with the help of modernized orthodoxy, checked, in the sixth decade of the century, even the spread of Reform.

Hess responded to all these movements within Jewry, and in his book an echo of all tendencies and strivings is heard. In his *Rome and Jerusalem* will be found a characteristic estimate of all these struggling forces within Judaism at the time. He, however, in his enthusiastic manner, overestimates the value of Jewish science for the National revival. It did not fulfil his expectations. Jewish science, with the exception of the writings of Krochmal and Luzzato, has not contributed much to National regeneration. It remains for it to atone in the future for the unpardonable sin it committed in the past.

The Life of Hess

Moses Hess was born in Bonn, Germany, on the twenty-first of January, 1812. His father was a wealthy merchant and thoroughly orthodox in his opinions. On his mother's side, Hess descended from a line of Rabbis and Jewish scholars. His early education was imbued with the Jewish spirit and the religious zeal of his parents. At the age of nine, Hess was given into the custody of his grandfather, his parents having left Bonn for Cologne. The grandfather was a pious Jew of the old type, a Rabbi by degree, but not by profession, and by his conduct he left a very deep impression upon the young Hess and instilled in him the deep love for the Jewish people, which finally found its expression in *Rome and Jerusalem,* Hess speaks of his grandfather in the most glowing terms.

In 1830, at the age of eighteen, Hess entered the Bonn University. It seems, however, that he never received an academic degree, having left the University in the midst of his course of study. The Universities were at that time the center of the Liberal and Radical movements and tendencies. Young Hess was powerfully attracted by these tendencies, and devoted himself with the entire force of his fiery soul to the propagation of the Socialist movement.

This radical activity on the part of the young Hess led finally to a break between him and his conservative father, and, as a result, Hess left Germany for England. After a short stay, he went to Paris, whence, having spent his money, he returned to Germany, making his journey on foot, and was engaged for a time as a teacher in the village near Metz.

A reconciliation was effected between father and son, and for a short time Hess was employed in his father's business. But commercial pursuits did not harmonize with the spirit of the young enthusiast, nor were the relations between him and his father very cordial; and, consequently, the war between the two broke out anew. When Hess, in 1840, married Sybille Fritsch, a Christian girl of questionable reputation, the break between him and his father was complete and the two never met again.

Hess, after giving up his business career, devoted his entire energy to philosophical studies and socialistic activity. In 1887 he published his first work, entitled, *The Sacred History of Humanity,* by a Young Spinozist. In this work, Hess develops his Philosophy of History, which is, in its essence, a combined product of Spinozism and Hegelianism. This work was followed, in 1841, by a second volume. *The European Triarchy,* where he advocates an alliance between England, France and Germany, the three most civilized nations of Europe; the same idea is repeated by him in his *Rome and Jerusalem.*

Hess was actively engaged, at the time, in the propaganda of Socialism and became one of the leaders of the radical movement. He was a contributor to all the Socialistic publications, especially the *Rhenische Zeitung,* of whose editorial staff he seems to have been a member. But such liberal publications were objectionable to the reactionary authorities and were soon forbidden by order of the police. The Socialists, together with the Radicals, were then forced to publish their works and periodicals in Switzerland. Such a periodical publication was *Ein und Zwanzig Bogen aus der Schweitz*—all works above twenty sheets were free from censorship—where a long article by Hess, under the name *The Philosophy of Action* was published. This article raised the philosophical standard of Hess in the eyes of his fellow-workers. Hess endeavors, in this article, to elaborate a system of philosophical Anarchism, declaring that the individual and the concrete is the only reality of the Idea, and vigorously denouncing all abstract generalities. The fundamental idea of the essay is, that the individual must have absolute freedom of action. This outburst of Individualism on the part of Hess, not only won him the displeasure of the socialist leaders, such as Marx and Engels, but did not harmonize with his own social nature and tendencies; he therefore modified his conception of egoism and socialized it. The highest development of the Ego, according to him, is when a man recognizes social life as his own. A direct result of his new teaching was his vigorous participation in the Communistic movement. In 1845, Hess engaged in propagating the Communistic idea and founding societies devoted to its realization, an occupation which led Arnold Ruge to describe him as "The Communist Rabbi Moses."

His communistic activity, however, was soon curtailed. Hess, coming more and more under the influence of Marx, adopted his views and began to preach the gospel of Economic Socialism. In his articles published in the subsequent year 1846 in Marx's *Jahrbuecher,* he advocated class struggle and declares himself a champion of the proletariat, Marx however, could not forgive Hess for his enthusiasm and warmth, and often denounced him. Even in the *Commumst Manifesto,* he directed some bitter shafts at him, calling him a dreamer and phantasist.

In 1847, Hess went to Brussels, and for a time contributed to the *Deutsche Brussiler Zeitung.* From Brussels he went to Paris. Meanwhile, however, the Revolution of 1848 broke out and Hess hastened to return to Germany, taking an active part in the armed resistance of the people. The following year, when reaction set in, Hess, among others, was condemned to death. For a time he wandered about aimlessly, attempting to settle in Geneva and Antwerp; but the Prussian government, demanding his extradition, made his stay unsafe, and he finally went, in 1853, to Paris, where he lived for the greater part of his remaining days.

The sixth decade of the nineteenth century was a period of reaction and conservatism in Germany. The revolutionary movement had spent its force in the attempted Revolution of 1848, and autocracy, regaining its strength, ruled with a mailed fist, though gloved in constitutional form. Many of the former revolutionary and liberal leaders, now in exile, despaired of ever carrying out their plan of a social change by means of revolution, and devoted themselves to other pursuits. Among them was Hess, who, during the eight years of his stay in Paris, from 1852 to 1860, occupied himself with the study of the physical and biological sciences, especially anatomy and anthropology. Arnold Ruge, the German philosopher and liberal, who was living in Paris at the time, scoffed at Hess's devotion to science and his forsaking of the ideal, and accused him of becoming an adherent of imperialism, but Hess was not swayed by these strictures.

These studies mark the turning point in Hess's mental attitude. Delving in Ethnology, Hess was convinced that the doctrine of Cosmopolitanism, which preaches the abolition of national landmarks and the fusing of humanity into one motley mass, has no scientific basis. He learned that Humanity consists of a group of nations, each distinct in physical type and mental peculiarities, and that these distinctions are not artificial, but primal and inherent. Hess then began to reflect about the fate and future of his own nation, which he had never entirely forgotten, but, as he himself says, his energies were temporarily diverted to what he at that time considered a greater and more important subject of attention—the European Proletariat. The result of these reflections was his *Rome and Jerusalem.* Hess carried into his new occupation, the preaching of Jewish Nationalism, the same fire and enthusiasm which animated his socialistic writings and activities and, naturally, the appearance of his book made a strong impression upon his contemporaries.

A champion of the Jewish National movement, Hess did not cease to be an ardent party socialist, and in 1863 went back to Germany for a short time and participated in propaganda work, under the direction of Lasalle. But it seems that his old zeal was gone, for he soon returned to Paris and devoted himself once more to his scientific studies, and also to Jewish studies. During the succeeding years he contributed frequently to socialistic periodicals, and also to Jewish publications, among which were the *Archives Israelites* and Graetz's *Monatsschrift fuer das Wissenschaft des Judenthums.*

At the outbreak of the Franco-Prussian War, Hess, as a Prussian subject, was exiled from Paris. And yet, this act did not embitter him against France, but, on the contrary, he grieved deeply at France's defeat. To give vent to his feeling, he published a book which he called *The Defeated Nation* in which he advocated an alliance of all nations against Prussianized Germany. After peace was established, he returned to Paris and to his scientific studies. Through his constant wandering and travel his health had become undermined and, after a few years of quiet work, he died in 1875, at the age of sixty-three. At his own request, he was buried in the family plot at Dietz on the Rhine. His wife, who survived him, published the first volume of his *Dynamic Matter,* in 1877.

THE PHILOSOPHY OF HESS

Hess is not a systematic thinker. He never endeavored to develop his view of the world

8

and life on the basis of fixed principles in logical sequence, but presented them in rather confused form. Yet the principles are there and have a direct relation to his views on Nature, Life, History and Judaism. Hess, as we have seen, wrote many works, but the latest of his productions, *Rome and Jerusalem*, in spite of its modest size, constitutes his *Magnum Opus*. In it we find a summary of his views on all grave questions in their most perfected form. The ideas expressed in it are valuable, not only as a foundation of the philosophy of Jewish Nationalism, but also as a contribution to human thought in general. With Hess, Judaism is not an isolated phenomenon of civilization, the expression of the spirit of a small people, but the most important constituent of the spiritual expression of Humanity. Hess raised Judaism to the dignity of a world philosophy, which has for its aim the elevation and perfection not only of the Jewish people, but of the entire human genus. His view of Judaism, however, is only a part of a general philosophical conception of Nature and life, a systematic exposition of the principles of which will help to elucidate it and enhance its value.

The fundamental principle of Hess's thought is what he terms "the genetic view." It is based on the teaching of Spinoza, of which he was a devoted follower. Hess, though influenced greatly by Hegel and the post-Hegelian philosophy, especially by that of Feuerbach, always remained a Spinozist, yet his teaching extends far beyond that of Spinoza, and is more adaptable to life, and more fruitful as a social factor. According to his view, the world, in spite of its multiplicity and variety of phases, is a unity. There is no place in it for a dualism of matter and spirit or other divisions; it is all one, —an undivided whole; the multiplicity in the universe is only apparent, the various unfoldings of the basic unity. Behind this unity there is the all-embracing force which unifies the phenomena of the universe—the Creator or God. God is not outside of the world but within it, its essence and substance. He, the all-unifying force, the Creator, expresses himself in all multiple phenomena of Nature and life, and thus creates them, making the entire world a created one

Hess's emphasis of creation gives to his philosophy an entirely new aspect, far exceeding in importance that of Spinoza. Spinoza, though employing the word creation, never conceived God as a real Creator, but endorses the mechanical view of the world, which sees in the universe a huge machine, working according to fixed laws, without aim and purpose. Hess, on the contrary, protests bitterly against this mechanical conception, and sees in the world a constant tendency toward creation, namely, the forming of things anew. The life of the world is not a mere blind operation of forces, but a development with a purpose and aim which will finally be realized. This aim is the harmony of all antagonistic elements, the reconciliation of all opposing forces, and the final peaceful cooperation of all for perfection and development. In this conception of reconciliation Hess shows the influence of Hegel's philosophy or *Synthesis,* which sees in the world of thought and life a constant process of opposition and reconciliation; but he employed it to better advantage than the master.

The creative force of the universe is a vital force, and the entire universe a live being which is divided into three life spheres: the cosmic, organic and social or the human. There are no hard and fast lines separating them, but they are all parts of a great whole, one creative force called them into being. The world is all movement; there is nothing stable in it; all things were formed anew. Hess does not believe in the eternity of matter, nor in the constancy of atoms. The atoms were created as all other things in this world and are subject to growth and decay. Atoms are only centers of gravity from which creation proceeds, and corresponding to them, in other spheres, are the germs in the organic, and revelations of creative ideas in the social.

Hess believes that this genetic conception is the real Jewish conception and points to the Biblical theory of creation. He was certainly right in his assertions. To look upon the world as a process of becoming and upon the creative force as vital, is a primary quality of Jewish thought and is best illustrated in Bergson. Comparing the view of Hess with that of the brilliant French-Jewish philosopher, we are struck with the similarity. Bergson, like Hess, struggles against the mechanical view of the world, and teaches a creative evolution constantly forming new productions, which are incalculable beforehand. Like Hess, he teaches the unity of the vital force which, though dividing itself into different forms, remains essentially one. There are undoubtedly differences between the two, but the fundamentals are the same with both of them; and, from a practical point of view, Hess's conception is far deeper and more fertile. Hess applies his philosophic thought to the social world, while Bergson remains in the middle of the road.

On the basis of the principles laid down by him in his view of the world, Hess constructed his philosophy of history. History, which embraces the social sphere of life is, according to him, not subordinate to Nature but on a par with it; it is dominated by the same laws and permeated with the same unified creative force. God reveals himself in history no less than in Nature; in this, he reminds us of the first Jewish national philosopher, Halevi,[1] and there is a divine plan in human affairs which is gradually unfolding itself in time.

Hess, like all thinkers of his time, was influenced in his conception of history by Hegel, whose principles he applied. History, like Nature, is a constant development, and is, of course, dominated by law, yet human freedom is preserved by the consciousness of our action. The development of history goes on in *dialectic* form, namely, forces opposing each other in earlier historical epochs are ultimately reconciled by a new synthetic epoch. Hess, viewing history as a part of the universal scheme, sees in its development an analogy to the development of Nature. In the former, as in the latter, there are three periods: rise, growth, and maturity, and there is also a corresponding similarity between the periods of these two spheres, which he elaborates fancifully in the tenth letter. The difference lies in this: that while Nature has already entered upon the third phase of its development, history is still striving toward it. Hess employs, as the means of conveying his ideas, the Biblical conception of Sabbath, which signifies "rest" as well as "completion." Nature has already attained its Sabbath, but History is yet to attain it. The Sabbath of history, the period of maturity of human development, is the Messianic era of the Prophets. It is a time when all opposing and struggling forces of the social sphere will be harmonized and men will become morally free. But in order to comprehend the full significance of Hess's historical conception and his grand vision of the future, we must understand his view of Society and its strivings. In his youth, when, in response to the impulses of his warm heart, he threw himself in the Socialist movement in order to attempt to alleviate human misery, Hess had no definite conception of human Society. He was swayed too often by different motives. Social life to him was only a constant antagonism between the collective body of society as a whole and its individual constituent members. Human history, he says somewhere in his writings, is a struggle actuated by two motives, egoism and love. In other words, there are two forces in Society, the disintegrating one, egoism, and the cementing force which binds one human being to the other, love. Hess always retained his belief in love as a moral factor and opens his book *Rome and Jerusalem* with a eulogy of it. As an escape from this eternal struggle, he proposed Communism, a state of Society which is bound to curb egoism and foster love. For a time, he swayed to Individualism. Under the

[1]See the writer's article on Halevi in *The American Hebrew,* Novemeber 10, 1916.

influence of Feuerbach and Bauer, he wrote his *Philosophy of Action*, which advocated the freedom of the individual. But, even then, he was not an egoist. Later, again, under the influence of Marx, he became more a class-struggle socialist. But in all these social changes of his, Hess conceived Society only as an aggregate of individuals.

It was only later, as a result of his anthropological studies, that Hess came to the conclusion that Society is not a mere abstract idea but is composed of definite subdivisions known as races, each of which has definite hereditary mental and physical traits which are unchangeable. He then formed his organic conception of Society, entirely independently of Spencer, which is the corner-stone of his social and Jewish philosophy. Society, according to this conception, is an organic body composed of organs, the races. Each of these organs or races has a different function to perform for the benefit of the whole. It is in the performance of this function that the purpose of existence of the organ is realized; and there exists in every organ a natural tendency to perform the function.

Hess developed an elaborate historical scheme, according to which every historical race had or has a certain mission or function to perform. The important places in this scheme are reserved by him for the two antithetical nations, the Greeks and the Jews. To the Greeks, the world presented multiplicity and variety; to the Jews, unity; the former conceived Nature and life as *being*, namely, as an accomplished thing; the latter, as *becoming*, as a thing constantly being created. The Greeks, like Nature, which they represented, had reached their aim in life and had, therefore, disappeared from the world. The Jews, on the other hand, representing History, the constantly striving force, are still in existence, endeavoring to carry out their aim, to bring about in this sphere of social life the historical Sabbath, namely, the harmony of all social forces.

Judaism is a historical religion, a religion which has for its field of operation the social sphere, and which has discovered God in history, namely, the creative and reconciling principle in the life of humanity. The most characteristic point of Judaism, says Hess, in one of his later articles,[2] is that it placed before human history its highest goal, the realization of universal law in Society. Judaism, he says in another place, is a humanitarian religion. According to its teachings, the life of the human genus is an organic process; it began with the family of the individual and will finally end with a family of nations. This, then, is the Jewish mission or function in Society, to realize the teachings of its great religion in practical life. The Jewish nation belongs to the creative organs of humanity. The Jews have taught humanity true religion, a religion which is neither materialistic nor spiritualistic, which has for its aim, unlike Christianity, not the salvation of the individual in the other world, but the perfection of social life in this world. And it is this function which they have to discharge to create for humanity new social values.

This function of Israel which, as a member of a great organism of Society, he is to perform, cannot be discharged anywhere else but in Palestine, where he will again be a nation possessing his own soil, a fundamental condition for living a regular normal social life. The regeneration of Judaism and Jewry is impossible in exile where it lacks the soil, the basis of a political life, and where there exists constant fear of disintegration. In exile, the Jews are unfruitful in all spheres, spiritually and economically. Jewish economic life, no matter how prosperous it may be in some countries, is abnormal; it lacks a basis, the soil; the Jews, therefore, cannot be creators and are only middlemen. It is only in their own land, where they will be able to produce new economic and social values, that they will continue to develop their greatest creation—Religion, which as a moral force will exert great influence upon

[2] *Die Einheit des Judenthums innerhalb der heutigen Religiosen Anarchie,* in the *Monatsschrift,* 1869.

humanity and thus bring about the realization of social harmony. In his attempt to lay the foundations of a positive view of Jewish life, Hess devoted considerable space to negative criticism of existing conceptions of Jewish life. His bitterest attacks are directed against the reformers and assimilators who deny Jewish nationality and substitute in its place an abstract indefinite teaching which they term, "Mission." Hess believes in a Jewish mission, but his mission is a natural function based on history and social life, while theirs is only a product of imagination and narrow vision. He attacks their ignorance of Jewish history and the misconception of the nature of Judaism as well as of Society in general, and ridicules their self-assumed rôle as the teachers of the nations. Their Judaism is only an empty shell, after the most important principles have been abandoned by them. The Orthodox Jews have, in his opinion, a much higher and truer conception of Judaism. They have retained in their ceremonies and prayers the kernel of Nationalism and the desire for Jewish restoration. Yet even they do not satisfy him entirely. Their inactivity and fossilized state irritate him. But he is optimistic. He believes that the spirit of regeneration will revive them and that they will finally furnish the material for a great National Movement. Hess also laid great hopes on Jewish science and expected it to become a great factor in the Jewish revival.

Hess developed a practical plan for the realization of his dream of Jewish restoration. He advocated the colonization of Palestine and the foundation of a Jewish Colonization Association. He dreamed that Jews, having been settled on the road to India and China, will become the mediators between Asia and Europe. For political support, he looked to his beloved France, the embodiment of freedom and the champion of oppressed nations. But he also dreamed of a Jewish Congress, demanding the support of the Powers for the purchase of Palestine, a dream quite prophetic in view of recent developments. He also foresaw a political situation resembling in its features the present state of affairs created by the war; he called it the last struggle between reaction and freedom. In some of his articles there are strikingly modern features.

Some of the dreams of this great visionary have partly come true. Let us gather confidence from the words of this modern seer, and hope that the glorious vision he foresaw for Israel will be realized in the coming period of history.

M. W.

Author's Preface

From the time that Innocent III[1] evolved the diabolical plan to destroy the moral stamina of the Jews, the bearers of Spanish culture to the world of Christendom, by forcing them to wear a badge of shame on their garments, until the audacious kidnapping of a Jewish child from the house of his parents, which occurred under the government of Cardinal Antonelli, Papal Rome symbolizes to the Jews an inexhaustible well of poison. It is only with the drying-up of this source that Christian German Anti-Semitism will die from lack of nourishment.

With the disappearance of the hostility of Christianity to culture, there ceases also its animosity to Judaism; with the liberation of the Eternal City on the banks of the Tiber, begins the liberation of the Eternal City on the slopes of Moriah; the renaissance of Italy heralds the rise of Judah.[2] The orphaned children of Jerusalem will also participate in the great regeneration of nations, in their awakening from the lethargy of the Middle Ages, with its terrible nightmares.

Springtime in the life of nations began with the French Revolution. The year 1789 marks the Spring equinox in the life of historical peoples. Resurrection of nations becomes a natural phenomenon at a time when Greece and Rome are being regenerated. Poland breathes the air of liberty anew and Hungary is preparing itself for the final struggle of liberation. Simultaneously, there is a movement of unrest among the other subjected nations, which will ultimately culminate in the rise of all the peoples oppressed both by Asiatic barbarism and European civilization against their masters, and, in the name of a higher right, they will challenge the right of the master nations to rule.

Among the nations believed to be dead and which, when they become conscious of their historic mission, will struggle for their national rights, is also Israel—the nation which for two thousand years has defied the storms of time, and in spite of having been tossed by the currents of history to every part of the globe, has always cast yearning glances toward Jerusalem and is still directing its gaze thither. Fortified by its racial instinct and by its cultural and historical mission to unite all humanity in the name of the Eternal Creator, this people has conserved its nationality, in the form of its religion and united both inseparably with the memories of its ancestral land.

No modern people, struggling for its own fatherland, can deny the right of the Jewish people to its former land, without at the same time undermining the justice of its own strivings.

But while the unprejudiced stranger considers the problem of Jewish Nationalism a timely one, it appears to cultured German Jews unreasonable. For it is in Germany that the difference between the Jewish and German races is emphasized and used both by the reactionary as well as by the liberal Anti-Semite as a cloak for their Judæophobia. It is there that the existence of Jewish nationality is still employed as an argument against the granting of practical and civil rights to the Jews. And this in Germany, where the Jews, from the time of Mendelssohn, in spite of their participation in all cultural and moral movements and their notable contribution to

[1]Innocent III, Pope from 1198 to 1216, was distinguished for his cruel hatred toward the Jews. At his instigation, the fourth Lateran Council adopted a Resolution urging the Christian Princes to force the Jews to wear a distinctive badge on their garments.——*Translator*.

[2]At the time when Hess wrote these lines, Italy, under the leadership of Garibaldi, was struggling to wrest Rome from the Papal government and annex it to the new unified Kingdom. The remarks in regard to Poland and Hungary are also explained by the events of the times.——*Translator*.

these fields, and notwithstanding their continual disavowal of Jewish national culture and their painstaking exertions to Germanize themselves, have striven in vain to obtain equal rights. But what brother did not obtain from brother, what was not granted by man to man, will be given by a people to a people, by a nation to a nation. No nation can be indifferent to the fact that in the coming European struggle for liberty it may have another people as its friend or foe.

The voices that are heard from various parts of the world, demanding the national regeneration of Israel, find justification, first of all, in the Jewish cult, in the national character of Judaism, and, even more, in the general process of development of humanity and its obvious results, and finally, in the present situation of human life.

In the series of letters that follow, the author has emphasized primarily the first mentioned, namely, the *inner* justification. In doing this he has been impelled to denounce the fantastic illusions of the rationalists and philanthropists who deny the national character of the Jewish religion, either on principle or for material reasons. But he must protest as vigorously against the dogmatic fanatics who, not being able to develop our historic religion along modern lines, have sought shelter under the wings of ignorance, so as to avoid a struggle with the deductions of science and criticism. He is thus preparing the way for the coming peace, which is daily breaking in upon the strife that is now raging between Reform and Orthodoxy.

Thanks to recent labors of Jewish scholars and the portrayal of Jewish life by talented novelists and poets, our national historical faith has found numerous adherents even among those to whom but recently enlightenment meant the falling away from Judaism. The field of Jewish science is common to reformers and to the orthodox alike. The inner motives, which in the course of the series of letters demonstrate the necessity and possibility of the national regeneration of Israel, are developed from the point of view of modern Jewish science.

"The history of the Post-talmudic Period," says the famous Jewish historian,[3] "still possesses a national character; it is by no means merely a creed or church history." "As the history of a people," he continues, "our history is far from being a mere chronicle of literary events or church history; why, therefore, characterize it as such? The literature and religious development, just as the tragic martyrdom, are only incidents in the life history of the people, not its substance."

Historical criticism now takes the place of the former method of rationalism employed by the Reformers, who wanted to separate the national from the religious in Judaism. They did not recognize the fountain of life, whence flowed our entire literature, Talmudic as well as Biblical. So much did they mistake the origin and cause of our literature that they considered that great organic creation, the Talmud, as representing merely the ever-changing result of an attempt to accommodate the life of the people to ever-changing conditions and environments.

Many who have emancipated themselves from dry orthodoxy have recently manifested in their studies a deepening conception of national Judaism; and have thus brought about the banishment of that superficial rationalism which was the cause of a growing indifference to things Jewish and which finally led to a total severance from Judaism. But we find, on the other hand, among the nationalistic ranks, rabbis, such as I used to meet in my younger days, who do not fall behind the Reformers in science and knowledge. The new seminaries, modeled after the Breslau school, which have been founded in every large Jewish center, ought to make it their aim to bridge the gap between the nihilism of the Reformers, which never learned anything, and the stanch

[3]Graetz, *History of the Jews*, German edition, Vol. 5, Introduction, p. 3.

conservatism of the orthodox, which never forgot anything. A mild, reviving breeze blows from the direction of such places where, a few years ago, Orthodoxy, on the one hand, threatened to freeze every movement, and Reform, on the other, as a destructive simoom, was about to burn up everything and sweep all vestiges of the ancient religion before it.

The general history of social and political life, as well as the national movement of modern nations, will be drawn upon, so as to throw light upon the undischarged function of Judaism. These sources will be utilized, furthermore, to demonstrate that the present political situation demands the establishment of Jewish colonies at the Suez Canal and on the banks of the Jordan. And, finally, these illustrations will be employed to point out the hitherto neglected fact, that behind the problems of nationality and freedom there is a still deeper problem which cannot be solved by mere phrases, namely, the race question, which is as old as history itself and which must be solved before attempting the solution of the political and social problems.

In order to anticipate unjustifiable criticism of my views by followers of the theory of German race Chauvinism, as well as by those Jews whose philosophy has not sufficiently progressed, I have thought it necessary to collect the ideas bearing on the subject, which are scattered through the letters, into one place, the epilogue. The epilogue, as well as the notes, is the right place for a more lengthy philosophical discussion and scientific demonstration of the principles which have been referred to somewhat superficially in the letters themselves.

First Letter

The return home—Jewish women—The source of the historical religion— Family love—Mater dolorosa.

After an estrangement of twenty years, I am back with my people. I have come to be one of them again, to participate in the celebration of the holy days, to share the memories and hopes of the nation, to take part in the spiritual and intellectual warfare going on within the House of Israel, on the one hand, and between our people and the surrounding civilized nations, on the other; for though the Jews have lived among the nations for almost two thousand years, they cannot, after all, become a mere part of the organic whole.

A thought which I believed to be forever buried in my heart, has been revived in me anew. It is the thought of my nationality, which is inseparably connected with the ancestral heritage and the memories of the Holy Land, the Eternal City, the birthplace of the belief in the divine unity of life, as well as the hope in the future brotherhood of men.

For a number of years this half-strangled thought stirred within my breast and clamored for expression. I lacked the strength to swerve suddenly from my beaten track, which seemed to be so far from the road of Judaism, to a new path which had unfolded itself before me in the hazy distance, in vague and dim outline.

Is it mere chance, that whenever I stand at a new turn in my life, there appears in my path an unhappy woman, who imparts to me daring and courage to travel the unknown road?

Oh, how stupid are those who minimize the value of woman's influence upon the development of Judaism! Was it not said of the Jews, that they were redeemed from Egypt because of the merit of the pious women, and that the future redemption will be brought about through them?[1]

It was only when I saw you in anguish and sorrow that my heart opened and the cover of my slumbering, national feeling was thrown off. I have discovered the fountain whence flows your belief in the eternity of the spirit.

Your infinite soul-sorrow, expressed on the death of one dear to you, brought about my decision to step forth as a champion of the national renaissance of our people. Such love which, like maternal love, flows out of the very life-blood and yet is as pure as the divine spirit; such infinite love for family can have its seat only in a Jewish heart. And this love is the natural source whence springs the higher, intellectual love of God which, according to Spinoza, is the highest point to which the spirit can rise. Out of this inexhaustible fountain of family love have the redeemers of humanity drawn their inspiration.

"In thee," says the divine genius of the Jewish family, "shall all the families of the earth be blessed."[2] Every Jew has within him the potentiality of a Messiah and every Jewess that of a *Mater dolorosa*.

---

[1] *Cf.* Note I at end of book.
[2] Genesis xii, 3.

SECOND LETTER

Thoughts on death and resurrection—Family tombs—Kindred souls—Jewish and Hindu saints—Schopenhauer—The end of days—The Sabbath of History.

Both sorrow and joy are contagious. You, my friend, have imbued me with your thoughts on death and resurrection. Heretofore, I have never visited a cemetery, but now the place holds an attraction for me. For the first time, since the untimely death of my mother, I visited the place where she lies buried and where later, during my absence from home, they laid my father to rest. I had forgotten the prayer usually read by Jews over the graves of their departed, and in ignorance my lips murmured the passage from the second of the eighteen benedictions: "Thou, O Lord, art mighty forever, thou restorest the dead to life..." when suddenly I noticed a lone tower on a nearby grave. Mechanically I picked it, carried it home with me and put it among my papers. Only later, I learned whose earthly remains rest beneath that mound. I knew then that the treasure, as you named the flower, belongs to you alone.

There are mystic relations between the living and the dead, though the nature and character of the communion will forever remain an unsolved riddle. More than your wonderful dreams, do my experiences in the waking state confirm the influence that the departed exert on the fate of those who remain behind.

"The departed souls continue to live in spirit."

And therefore do I love also death. But must I then hate life? Nay, I love life as well, only I love it in the sense the greatest thinker of the centuries, Spinoza, loved it. The more humanitarian, the holier, the more divine life is, the more does it appear that life and death are of equal value and equal worth.

The Jews alone were able to rise to that spiritual height, where life and death appear to be of equal value; and yet they never renounced life, but clung to it tenaciously. Already eighteen hundred years ago, a Jew, who has since become a redeemer among the gentiles, found an extra-mundane point of support, from which he wished to lift the world from its poles.[1]

The great teachers of the knowledge of God were always Jews. Our people not only created the noblest religion of the ancient world, a religion which is destined to become the common property of the entire civilized world, but continued to develop it, keeping pace with the progress of the human spirit. And this mission will remain with the Jews until the end of days, i.e., until the time when, according to the promise of our Prophets, the world will be filled with the knowledge of God. The "end of days," so often spoken of by the Prophets, is not to be understood to mean, as some misinterpret it, the end of the world, but it denotes the period when the development and education of humanity will reach their highest point.

We are on the eve of the Sabbath of History and should prepare for our last mission through a thorough understanding of our historical religion.

We cannot understand a single word of the Holy Scriptures, so long as we do not possess the point of view of the genius of the Jewish nation which produced these writing. Nothing is more foreign to the spirit of Judaism than the idea of the salvation of the individual which, according to the modern conception, is the corner-stone of religion. Judaism as never drawn any line of separation between and the family, the family and the nation, the nation and humanity as a whole, humanity and the cosmos,

[1] See Note II at end of book. Hess alludes here to the famous saying of Archimedes: "Give me a place to stand and I will move the earth."—*Translator.*

nor between creation and creator. Judaism has no other dogma but the teaching of the unity. But this dogma is with Judaism, not a mere fossilized and therefore barren belief, but a living, continually recreating principle of knowledge. Judaism is rooted in the love of the family; patriotism and nationalism are the flowers of its spirit, and the coming regenerated state of human Society will be its ripe fruit. Judaism would have shared the fate of other religions which were fossilized through their dogmas and which will finally disappear through the conflict with science, had it not been for the fact that religious teachings are the product of life. Judaism is not a passive religion, but an active life factor which has coalesced with the national consciousness into one organic whole. It is primarily the expression of a nationality whose history for thousands of years coincides with the history of the development of a humanity and the Jews are a nation which, having once acted as the leaven of the social world, is destined to be resurrected with the rest of civilized nations.

THIRD LETTER

Immortality—Rabbi Jochanan—Nachmanides—Messianic travails—Pater noster—Solidarity—The call of France and the rumbling of the reactionaries.

You wonder why it is that there is no mention of the doctrine of immortality in the Old Testament. The *Agadic* interpretations of verses, as well as the manipulations of certain Biblical passages by modern Jewish and Christian exegetes, which tend to infer from these verses and passages the belief in immortality, do not satisfy you, and rightly so. You argue, that if Moses and the Prophets had believed in a life beyond the grave, in the Christian sense, they would have stated the fact as explicitly as did the writers of the New Testament, and would not have limited reward and punishment to the life of this world alone. I do not deny the fact that there is no mention of immortality in the Old Testament. But if you reproach our Holy Scriptures for passing over such an important doctrine in silence, you forget the viewpoint of the genius of the Jewish nation which produced these Scriptures. You overlook the point of view of our sacred history, namely, the genetic conception which never separated the individual from the race, the nation from humanity, and the created world from the Creator. You forget that the part of the Sacred Scriptures wherein there is no mention of immortality was written at a time when the Jewish nation was still in existence, and therefore there was no need of a belief in a resurrection. The Jewish belief in immortality is inseparable from the national-humanitarian Messianic idea. "It is only with the coming of the Messiah and the establishing of the Messianic kingdom that the purpose of creation will be accomplished," says R. Jochanan, one of the leading *Amoraim*. In another statement, he adds, that "all the beautiful visions of the Prophets refer only to the Messianic reign; but as regards the world to come, its character and nature is known to God alone."[1] Even in later Rabbinic Judaism, the Rabbis never separated the idea of a future world from the conception of the Messianic reign. Nachmanides insists; in contradiction to Maimonides; upon the identity of *Olam Habbo*, "the world to come," with the Messianic reign.

There was no necessity for Judaism to emphasize the eternity and indestructibility of the spirit, for its own history is nothing but the embodiment of this idea. It was only when Judaism was threatened with the possibility of national destruction, as early as the end of the period of the first Temple that along with the idea of national destruction and the hope of a national rebirth, there arose also the idea of the immortality of the individual. The Prophet Isaiah already draws a sharp line of distinction between those nations which are doomed to eternal death and Israel who is destined to be resurrected. The momentary death of Israel, the people of the spirit, is only the preliminary stage for a future eternal life. (Isa. xxvi, 14-19.)

Even in primitive Christianity, as long as it did not separate itself completely from Judaism and the historical cult, the Jewish conception still survived, according to which resurrection, the "Kingdom of Heaven," and the "world to come," are identical with the Messianic age, the rebirth of the Jewish nation. The coming of the reign of the spirit is heralded in the Gospels, and also in the famous prayer of Jewish origin, "*Pater Noster,*" "Our Father," as a definite event in the history of the Jews.

Even the latest expression of the Jewish genius concerning life and death, namely, the teaching of Spinoza, has nothing in common with the sickly atomistic conception of immortality, a conception which dissolves the unity of life either in a spiritualistic way or in a materialistic manner, and whose highest religious and moral principle is the

---

[1] For the references to the sayings of R. Jochanan, see Sanhedrin, 98b and 99a.—*Translator.*

21

egoistic maxim, "everyone for himself." No nation was ever so far from this egoistic principle as was the Jewish people. With the Jews, solidarity and social responsibility were always the fundamental principles of life and conduct.[2]

In the *Sayings of the Fathers*, the rule of bourgeois morality—"everyone for himself"—is severely condemned, and is declared to be a wicked rule of conduct.[3] In the teaching of Spinoza, as in the teaching of the Jewish saints, the individual is not treated as a separate entity, but as a part of a whole. According to Spinoza, eternity does not begin with our death, but always exists, is always present even as God himself.

Very few, indeed, possess the noble spirit which animated the Jewish saints. Most people are anxious to secure as much immortality as possible for themselves, and for themselves alone. True it is that the "end of days," when the knowledge of God will fill the earth, is still far off; yet we firmly believe that the time will come when the holy spirit of our nation will become the property of humanity and the earth will become a grand temple wherein the spirit of God will dwell. In the Bible, the reign of the spirit is declared to be a future event, and even long afterward people relegated these prophetic visions to the realm of the world to come—"*Olam Habbo*"—and did not connect them with the present life. Spinoza was the first to conceive the reign of the spirit as an existing thing, as a factor in the present life. It is true, the reign of the spirit exists already, but only as a germ of spiritual light. To develop this germ to its fullest possibilities, so that it will create social values, there labor, along with the Jewish people, the most intellectual, moral and creative of modern nations, namely Germany, France and England. These three nations have contributed greatly to the store of civilization, each its distinctive share. Germany has built the road to philosophy France has thrown open to all nations the way to social and political changes and improvements, and has also blazed the path of progress for the natural sciences. England, like Germany, has followed, slowly but surely, her own lead, namely, that of the progress and development of industry.

The Jews felt long ago that the struggle for regeneration waged by the nations, together with France, is their own cause, and have therefore everywhere joined, enthusiastically and voluntarily, the ranks of the followers of the political-social movements. "The time has arrived," says a well-known French democrat to the Jews, "when you should think less of others and more of yourselves, and commence to work for your own regeneration."[4] The latter, however, does not exclude the former. When I labor for the regeneration of my own nation, I do not thereby renounce my humanistic aspiration. The national movement of the present day is only another step on the road of progress which began with the French Revolution. The French nation has, since the great Revolution, been calling to the other nations for help. But the nations have turned a deaf ear to the voice from the distance and have lent a not unwilling ear to the tumult of reaction in their own midst. To-day, this roar deafens only the people in certain parts of Germany, those who, by dint of political trickery, are aroused to the pitch of

---

[2]The solidarity of the Jews covers also the *Shem*, i.e., the name of God. The Jewish law of solidarity: "All Israelites are responsible for one another," is expressed also in the form of *Kiddush Hashem*, the Sanctification of God's name; i.e., the Jew is urged to act in a more unselfish spirit than the law requires, and even to sacrifice his own interests and person, that he may thereby reflect glory upon the name of Judaism and all other Jews.

[3]Compare Note V at the end, where the opinion of the Rabbis in the *Sayings of the Fathers* about the various standards of conduct in relation to "mine and thine" are given in detail. In regard to the ordinary conception of common morality of "everyone for himself," it is said there: He who says: "What is mine is mine and what is thine is thine, his is a neutral character;—some say this is a character like that of Sodom." (*Ethics*, V. 13)

Another saying *Aboth*, which is also found in *Aboth d' R. Nathan* in an imperfect and contradictory form, admonishes us that we should not be like servants who serve for the sake of reward but like children who perform their duty because of the reverence inspired in them by the majesty of the father of all being. This teaching seems to be indifferent to the doctrine of immortality. (Compare Epilogue, 3.)

[4]See the extracts from the pamphlet: *The New Oriental Problem*, quoted in the eleventh letter.

enthusiasm for the kings and war lords. But the other nations hear and follow the call of France. The call has reached also our ancient nation, and I would unite my voice with that of France, that I may at least warn my racial brothers in Germany against listening to the loud noise of the reactionaries.[5]

FOURTH LETTER

German Anti-Semitism—Patriotic romanticists and philosophic book-dealers—Otto Wigand—Berthold Auerbach—Moleschott—Dr. Gallavardin—Reform and Jewish noses —A Photographic picture—Hebrew prayers—Patriotism—My grandfather—Our Mother Rachel—National sorrow—The Black Sabbath.

It seems that German education is not compatible with our Jewish national aspirations. Had I not once lived in France, it would never have entered my mind to interest myself with the revival of Jewish nationality. Our views and strivings are determined by the social environment which surrounds us. Every Living, acting people, like every active individual, has its special field. Indeed, every man, every member of the historical nations, is a political, or as we say at present, a social animal; yet within this sphere of the common social world, there are special places reserved by Nature for individuals according to their particular calling. The specialty of the German of the higher class, of course, is his interest in abstract thought; and because he is too much of a universal philosopher, it is difficult for him to be inspired by national tendencies. "Its whole tendency," my former publisher, Otto Wigand, once wrote to me, when I showed him an outline of a work on Jewish national aspirations, "is contrary to my pure human nature."

The "pure human nature" of the Germans is, in reality, the character of the pure German race, which rises to the conception of humanity in theory only, but in practice it has not succeeded in overcoming the natural sympathies and antipathies of the race. German antagonism to Jewish national aspiration has a double origin, though the motives are really contrary to each other. The duplicity and contrariety of the human personality, such as we can see in the union of the spiritual and the natural, the theoretical and the practical sides, are in no other nation so sharply marked in their points of opposition as in the German. Jewish national aspirations are antagonistic to the theoretical cosmopolitan tendencies of the German. But in addition to this, the German opposes Jewish national aspirations because of his racial antipathy, from which even the noblest Germans have not as yet emancipated themselves. The publisher, whose "pure human" conscience revolted against publishing a book advocating the revival of Jewish nationality, published books preaching hatred to Jews and Judaism without the slightest remorse, in spite of the fact that the motive of such works is essentially opposed to the "pure human conscience." This contradictory action was due to inborn racial antagonism to the Jews.[1] But the German, it seems, has no clear conception of his racial prejudices; he sees in his egoistic as well as in his spiritual endeavors, not German or Teutonic, but "humanitarian tendencies"; and he does not know that he follows the latter only in theory, while in practice he clings to his egoistic ideas.

Progressive German Jews, also, seem to think that they have sufficient reason for turning away from the Jewish national movement. My dear old friend, Berthold Auerbach, is disappointed with me, just as much as my former publisher, though not on the ground of "pure human conscience." He complains bitterly about my attitude and finally exclaims: "Who appointed you as a prince and judge over us?"[2] It seems that on account of the hatred which surrounds him on all sides, the German Jew is

---

[1] See Note III at end of book.

[2] Exodus ii, 14. Auerbach gave me great satisfaction by quoting the biblical verse in the original Hebrew. He recognizes my right to express my Jewish sympathies and feelings, to which he is not averse. But he claims that such an expression should bear more of the character of personal sentiment and not be made public. Such action, according to him, is dangerous and can become a "fire brand" in the hands of the Anti-Semites.

25

determined to estrange himself from Judaism as far as possible, and endeavors even to deny his race. No reform of the Jewish religion, however extreme, is radical enough for the educated German Jew. But the endeavors are vain. Even conversion itself does not relieve the Jew from the enormous pressure of German Anti-Semitism. The German hates the Jewish religion less than the race; he objects less to the Jews' peculiar beliefs than to their peculiar noses. Neither reform, nor conversion, nor emancipation throw open to the Jew the gates of social life, hence their anxiety to deny their racial descent. Moleschott, in his *Physiological Sketches* (p. 251), tells how the son of a converted Jew used to spend hours every morning at the looking-glass, comb in hand, endeavoring to straighten his curly hair, so as to give it a more Teutonic appearance. But as little as the "radical" Reform movement—an appellation which characterizes it so well, inasmuch as it lays the ax at the root of Judaism and its national historical cult— accomplished its aim, so little will the tendency of some Jews to deny their racial descent fulfill their purpose. Jewish noses cannot be reformed, and the black, wavy hair of the Jews will not change through conversion into blond, nor can its curves be straightened out by constant combing. The Jewish race is one of the primary races of mankind that has retained its integrity, in spite of the continual change of its climatic environment, and the Jewish type has conserved its purity through the centuries.

On the western mountain slope which encloses the City of the Dead, at Thebes, in Egypt, there still exists the tomb of one of the ancient architects, who supervised the construction of the king's buildings, on which are depicted reliefs of all the works constructed under his direction. Here we can see how the obelisks were erected, the sphinxes hewn out of the rock, the palaces built, as well as how all the preliminary labor was performed. Here are scenes representing white Asiatic slaves making bricks, many of which are piled up near the building, while other slaves are carrying stones away. At a little distance from the group of laboring slaves stands the overseer with raised whip in his hand. The tomb was built, according to the inscription, about the time of Moses, and in the reliefs of the Asiatic slaves there is a resemblance to the present Jewish type.[3] Later Egyptian monuments, likewise, show Jewish reliefs which strikingly resemble our modern Jews.

The Jewish race, which was so hard pressed and almost destroyed by many nations of antiquity, would have disappeared long ago, in the sea of the Indo-Germanic nations, had it not been endowed with the gift of retaining its peculiar type under all circumstances and of reproducing it. If Judaism owes its immortality to the remarkable religious productivity of the Jewish genius, this genius owes its existence to the fertility of the Jewish race. The words of the Bible, "But the more they afflicted them, the more they multiplied and the more they spread abroad and the land was filled with them," which were written of the Jews in Egypt, are true of them also during the third exile.

Of the predominance of the Jewish type in cases of intermarriage with members of the Indo-Germanic race, I can quote an example from my own experience. It is a well-known fact, that in unions between members of the Mongolian, with those of the Indo-Germanic race, the Mongolian type predominates; for example, the Russian nobles, who have little Mongolian blood in their veins, yet display in their physiognomy Mongolian features even to the present day.[4] Among my friends there is a Russian nobleman who, like all the Russian boyars; betrays his mixed descent, the Mongolian, by his features, and the Indo-Germanic, by his fine intellect. This friend

[3] *Sinai and Golgotha*, by F. A. Strauss, p. 69.
[4] Russia was overrun in the thirteenth century by Mongolian hordes and for a time was subject to one of the Tartar kingdoms established on its borders. During this time the two races mingled freely, so that, as a result, the Mongolian type is quite prevalent among the Russians.—*Translator.*

married a Polish Jewess, by whom he had a number of sons, who all possess Jewish features in marked degree. As you see, my esteemed friend, Jews and Jewesses endeavor, in vain, to obliterate their descent through conversion or intermarriage with the Indo-Germanic and Mongolian races, for the Jewish type is indestructible. Nay more, the type is undeniable, even in its most beautiful representatives, where it approaches the ancient Greek type, and even surpasses it with its peculiar soul expression. Hence I was not surprised, when traveling through Antwerp, I showed an artist the beautiful picture known to you, that he, enthusiastically admiring the image that would have done credit to a Phidias, exclaimed: "I will wager that it is the picture of a Jewess."

The Jewish race, throughout the world, possesses the ability to acclimatize itself more than all other races. Just as in the native land of the Jews, Palestine, there grow plants of the southern and of the northern zones, so does this people, of the temperate clime, thrive in all zones. A French physician, Dr. Gallavardin, has demonstrated this physiological phenomenon by many statistical data, in his well-known work, *The Position of the Jews in the World.*

And just as it is impossible for me to entertain any prejudice against my own race, which has played such an important rôle in universal history and which is destined for a still greater one in the future, so it is impossible for me to show against the holy language of our fathers the antipathy of those who endeavor to eliminate Hebrew from Jewish life, and even supersede it by German inscriptions in the cemetery. I was always exalted by the Hebrew prayers. I seem to hear in them an echo of fervent pleadings and passionate entreaties, issuing from suffering hearts of a thousand generations. Seldom do these heart-stirring prayers fail to impress those who are able to understand their meaning. The most touching point about these Hebrew prayers is, that they are really an expression of the collective Jewish spirit; they do not plead for the individual, but for the entire Jewish race. The pious Jew is above all a Jewish patriot. The "new" Jew, who denies the existence of the Jewish nationality, is not only a deserter in the religious sense, but is also a traitor to his people, his race and even to his family. If it were true that Jewish emancipation in exile is incompatible with Jewish nationality, then it were the duty of the Jews to sacrifice the former for the sake of the latter. This point, however, may need a more elaborate explanation,[5] but that the Jew must be above all a Jewish patriot, needs no proof to those who have received a Jewish education. Jewish patriotism is not a cloudy Germanic abstraction, which dissolves itself in discussions about being and appearance, realism and idealism, but a true, natural feeling, the tangibility and simplicity of which require no demonstration, nor can it be disposed of by a demonstration to the contrary.

My grandfather once showed me some olives and dates, and remarked, with beaming eyes, "These were raised in *Eretz Yisroel.*" Everything that reminds the pious Jew of Palestine is as dear to him as the sacred relics of his ancestral house. It is customary that a bag containing earth from the Holy Land is put into the grave of every pious Jew. In this practice, however, as well as in the ritualistic use of the citron and palm branch which, like the bag of earth, are imported from Palestine at great expense, there is something more than the mere carrying out of a religious precept or the prompting of superstitious belief. All feast and fast days of the Jews, their deep piety and reverence for tradition, which almost apotheosizes everything Hebraic, nay even the entire Jewish cult, all have their origin in the patriotism of the Jewish nation. The Jewish "reformers," who have emancipated themselves from Jewish nationality, understand this quite well; they are therefore very careful in expressing their heartfelt opinions.

They find it more comfortable to take refuge in the falsehood of the dualistic theory, which sees in every natural and simple feeling, as well as in patriotism, a double essence—an ideal and a real. This dualistic theory is very useful, as it can be adjusted at well, either to the one point of view or to the other.

This false theory is of recent German invention and need not be taken seriously. Spinoza conceived Judaism to be grounded in Nationalism, and held that the restoration of the Jewish kingdom depends entirely upon the will and courage of the Jewish people. Even the rationalistic Mendelssohn did not know of a cosmopolitan Judaism. It is only in modern times that, for the purposes of obtaining equal rights, some German Jews denied the existence of Jewish nationality. Moreover, they have convinced themselves, contrary to the fact that the further existence of Judaism will not at all be threatened by the elimination of its innermost essence.

True, my dear friend, it is a fact which may even come to the attention of our German Jewish reformers, that the Jewish religion is, above all, Jewish patriotism. I always recall, with deep emotion, the scenes that I lived through when a child, at the house of my grandfather at Bonn, on the fast-day commemorating the destruction of Jerusalem. On the first day of the month of Ab, which is the first of the nine days preceding the eventful day, the sorrow which had been manifested since the beginning of the "three weeks," assumed a more perceptible form. Even the Sabbath day lost its festive character during these days of national mourning, and was named "the black Sabbath." My pious grandfather was one of those revered scholars who, though not using the Torah as a means of subsistence, yet possessed the title and knowledge of a rabbi. Every evening, at the close of his business day, he spent several hours in studying the Talmud and its commentaries. But in the "nine days" this study was interrupted, and instead be read with his grandchildren the stories and legends concerning the exile of the Jews from Jerusalem. The tears fell upon the snow-white beard of the stern old man as he read those stories, and we children, too, would cry and sob. I remember, especially, one particular passage which impressed us both deeply. It runs as follows:

"When the children of Israel were led into captivity by the soldiers of Nebuchadnezzar, their road lay past the grave of our Mother Rachel. As they approached the grave, a bitter wailing was heard. It was the voice of Rachel, weeping at the fate of her unhappy children."[6]

You can now discern clearly the source of the Jewish belief in immortality; it is the product of our remarkable family love. Our immortality extends back into the past as far as the Patriarchs, and in the future to Messiah's reign. It is the Jewish conception of the family which gave rise to the vivid belief in the continuity of the spirit in human history. This belief, which is one of the fairest blossoms of Judaism, the roots of which are to be found in Jewish family love and the trunk in Jewish patriotism, has, in the course of ages, shrunk to the belief in the atomistic immortality of the individual soul; and thus, torn from its roots and trunk, has withered and decayed. It is only in the Jewish conception of the family that the former living belief is still retained. When modern dualism of spirit and matter, the result of the separation of Christianity from Judaism, had found its highest expression in the works of the last Christian philosopher, Descartes, and had threatened to kill all unity of life, there arose again out of Judaism the belief in the existence of one eternal force in Nature and history. This belief acted as a bulwark against spiritual egoism, on the one hand, and materialistic individualism on the other.[7] Just as Christian dualism received its mortal

[6]Jeremiah xxxi, 14.
[7]The monistic teaching of Spinoza is here referred to by Hess.—*Translator.*

blow from the teachings of Spinoza, so does the existence of the ancient Jewish people, with its model family life, act as an antidote against this disease of dualism in practical life. Even today the wholesome influence of the Jewish family life is noticeable in literature, art and science. How much greater will that influence be when once again we create history and literature, when once more the Torah will go forth from Zion and the Word of the Lord from Jerusalem?[8]

---

[8]Micah iv, 1; Isaiah ii, 2. "But in the last days it shall come to pass that ... the Law shall go forth from Zion, and the word of the Lord from Jerusalem." It is an old prophecy, repeated in identical ords by various prophets, the echo of which reverberates throughout our entire history.

Retrospect—The Damascus Affair—A cry of anguish—Mamserbilbul, i.e., Blood Accusation—Hep, Hep—The escape into France—Arnold Ruge—Napoleon—An honest German—Teutomaniacs—Jefferson—Fatherlands and Sovereigns—Ubi bene ibi Patria —The Jewish incognito—The religion of death—Raise your standard high, my people.

Do I seriously believe in the redemption from exile? You ask this question, and also remind me that I have already expressed myself in my two earlier works, *The Sacred History of Humanity* and *The Triarchy of Europe,* as a believer in the fulfillment of the Messianic hope. You are certainly going far afield, esteemed friend, in holding me responsible not only for my present opinions, but also for those expressed long ago. Nevertheless, you are right, and I assume full responsibility for my ideas. But in order not to stray too far from the thought nearest to my heart into my own personal history, I will relate only a few of the most characteristic episodes of my past, which will elucidate my present attitude toward the national question.

Twenty years ago, when an absurd and false accusation against the Jews was imported into Europe from Damascus,[1] it evoked in the hearts of the Jews a bitter feeling of agony. Then it dawned upon me for the first time, in the midst of my socialistic activities, that I belong to my unfortunate, slandered, despised and dispersed people. And already, then, though I was greatly estranged from Judaism, I wanted to express my Jewish patriotic sentiment in a cry of anguish, but it was unfortunately immediately stifled in my heart by a greater pain which the suffering of the European Proletariat evoked in me.

With other nations, there is strife only among the various parties, but the Germans clash even when they belong to the same party. The members of my own party have made me loathe the aspirations of the Germans, and by their actions caused me to go into exile several years before the triumphant reaction changed it from a voluntary act into an involuntary one. Only a short time after the February revolution, I went to France and there I learned to know the people which, in the present century, is the foremost champion of social liberty. If this people submits at present to the iron dictatorship of kinghood, it is because the Emperor is true to his revolutionary descent,[2] not in word alone, but also in deed. The moment dynastic interests conflict with the aspirations and strivings of the French people, kinghood will disappear from the soil of France.

After the *coup d'etat* of the reaction,[3] I withdrew from politics and devoted myself exclusively to natural sciences. Old Dr. Arnold Ruge, a follower of the Young Hegelians,[4] was much shocked at my occupation, which he termed materialism; he could never forgive the "Communist Rabbi Moses" for his heresy in forsaking the "ideal." He hinted frequently, in his lectures at the German Museum, that this scientific materialism is in reality only Imperialism, but not of the German-Barbarossa type,[5] but only of the Romance-Bonapartistic stamp. What relation there is between the study of the natural sciences and Bonapartism, the old Ruge never explained

---

[1]This is the well-known ritual murder case of Damascus, usually referred to as the Damascus affair, of 1840. The number of accused Jews, as well as the inquisitorial methods applied in extorting a confession, attracted the attention of the leading Jews of Europe, including Sir Moses Montefiore and Isaac Cremieux, through whose efforts the Government of France and England finally intervened and obtained the release of the accused.—*Translator.*

[2]The Emperor of France at the time was Napoleon III, the nephew of Napoleon.—*Translator.*

[3]This refers to the crushing of the popular revolution in Germany by Prussia, in the year 1849.—*Translator.*

[4]Young Hegelianism is the name given to the radical interpretation of Hegel's philosophy. Its followers were mostly revolutionaries and socialists. Ruge was one of its principal leaders.—*Translator.*

clearly. Meanwhile, even since the beginning of the Italian War of Liberation, I discovered a real and strong relationship between my ethnological studies and the modern national movement, which received such a strong impetus since the war. I will, on a later occasion, relate to you some of the conclusions reached through these studies. Let it suffice for the present, to say that these studies convinced me of the inevitable ultimate disappearance of any particular race dominance and the necessary regeneration of all oppressed peoples. First of all, it was my own Jewish people who, since that time, began to interest me and enchant me more and more. Images of my unfortunately brethren who surrounded me in my youth haunted my thoughts, and the long-suppressed feelings burst forth with fresh vigor. The pain and agony which, during the Damascus affair, was only a transient feeling, became now a dominating trait of my character and a lasting mood of my soul. No more did I seek to suppress the voice of my Jewish consciousness, but on the contrary, I carefully followed up its traces and was pleasantly surprised when I found; in my old manuscripts, a passage anticipating my present-day Jewish aspirations.

The following passage was written by me in the year 1840, during the time of the above-mentioned Damascus affair:

"The way and manner in which the persecution of the Jews in Europe, even in enlightened Germany, is looked upon, must necessarily cause a new point of departure in the Jewish life. This tendency demonstrates quite clearly that in spite of the degree of education to which the Occidental Jews have attained, there still exists a barrier between them and the surrounding nations, almost as formidable as in the days of religious fanaticism. Those of our brethren who, for purposes of obtaining emancipation, endeavor to persuade themselves, as well as others, that modern Jews possess no trace of a national feeling, have really lost their heads."[6] These men do not understand how it is possible that such a stupid, Mediæval legend, which was only too well known to our forefathers under the name of *Mamserbilbul,* should be given credence, even for a moment, in Nineteenth Century Europe. To our educated German Jews, the feeling of hatred toward the Jews displayed by the Germans has always remained an unsolved puzzle. Was not the entire effort of the German Jews, since the days of Mendelssohn, directed toward becoming wholly Germanized, to thinking and feeling as Germans? Have they not striven carefully to eradicate every trace of their ancient nationality? Have they not fought in the War of Liberation? Were they not Teutomaniacs and French devourers? Did we not chant but yesterday with Nicolas Becker, "They shall not possess it, the free German Rhine"? Did I myself not commit the unpardonable stupidity of sending a musical composition of this "German Marseillaise" to the author of this song?

And yet I had to feel, in a personal way, the same disappointment that German Jewry in general experienced after it had given repeated demonstration of its patriotic enthusiasm. I also had to experience the sad fact that the German to whom I sent my manuscript, glowing with patriotic emotion, not only responded to it in an icy tone,

---

[5]Frederick Barbarossa was Emperor of Germany from 1152 to 1189. His reign was marked by brilliancy, power and iron-handed ruling. His strong personality left a lasting impression upon the mind of the German people, so that he became the hero of a number of legends. He represents, therefore, to the German, the ideal type of a strong-handed Emperor.—*Translator.*

[6]The *Allgemeine Zeitung des Judenthums,* which is otherwise a progressive publication, complained bitterly at the time. "Europe," says this worthy publication, in one of its issues, "has spared the followers of the religion of Israel neither pain, nor tears, nor bitterness." Were the Jews only followers of a certain religious denomination, like the others, then it were really inconceivable that Europe, and especially Germany, where the Jews have participated in every cultural activity, "should spare the followers of the Israelitic confession neither pain, nor tears, nor bitterness." The solution of the problem, however, consists in the fact that the Jews are something more than mere "followers of a religion," namely, they are a race brotherhood, a nation, one which, unfortunately, whose existence is denied by its own children and which every street loafer considers it his duty to despise as long as it is homeless.

but as if to fill the cup of bitterness to the brim, wrote on the other side of his letter, in a disguised script, the words: "You are a Jew." I forgot, then, that the Germans, after the War of Liberation, not only discriminated against the Jews, their erstwhile comrades in arms against the French, but even persecuted them with the frequent cries of *Hep, Hep.* I, on the other hand, took Becker's *Hep, Hep,* as a personal insult, and accordingly wrote him a letter, not in a disguised script, making a few unpleasant remarks, which this honest German, who most likely felt ashamed of his rudeness, passed over in silence. To-day I could have apologized to this German poet, for, as I see clearly now, it was by no means intended as a personal insult. It is impossible for any man to be at the same time a Teutomaniac and a friend of the Jews, just as it is impossible to love, simultaneously, the German military rule and German democracy. The real Teutomaniacs of the Arndt and Jahn type will always be honest, reactionary conservatives. The Teutomaniac, in his love of the Fatherland, loves not the State but the race dominance. How, then, can he conceive the granting of equal rights to other races than the dominant one, when equality is still a Utopia for the large masses of Germany? The sympathetic Frenchman assimilates with irresistible attraction every foreign race element. Even the Jew is here a Frenchman. Jefferson said long ago, at the time of the American Revolution, that every man has two fatherlands, first his own and then France. The German, on the other hand, is not at all anxious to assimilate any foreign elements, and would be perfectly happy if he could possess all his fatherlands and dominions for himself. He lacks the primary condition of every chemical assimilative process, namely, warmth.

As long as the Jew submitted in silence to persecution and disgrace, considering it as a punishment of God, all the time confidently hoping for the future restoration of his nation, his pride was not impaired. His only care was to enable his race to reach that glorious future which would amply recompense it for all the suffering it had undergone in the past, when God will mete out punishment to the persecutors and enemies of Israel. Our enlightened Jews, however, possess this strong belief and vigorous hope no more. What good is emancipation to them? Of what avail is it that here and there a Jew rises to high office, when to the name "Jew" there is attached a stigma which every obscure journalist, every stupid fellow, can safely turn to account?

As long as the Jew endeavors to deny his nationality, while at the same time he is unable to deny his own individual existence, as long as he is unwilling to acknowledge that he belongs to that unfortunate and persecuted people, his false position must daily become more intolerable. Wherefore the illusion? The European nations have always considered the existence of the Jews in their midst as an anomaly. We shall always remain strangers among the nations. They may tolerate us and even grant us emancipation, but they will never *respect* us as long as we place the principle *ubi bene ibi patria* above our own great national memories. Though religious fanaticism may cease to operate as a factor in the hatred against the Jews in civilized countries, yet in spite of enlightenment and emancipation, the Jew in exile who denies his nationality will never earn the respect of the nations among whom he dwells. He may become a naturalized citizen, but he will never be able to convince the gentiles of his total separation from his own nationality. It is not the old-type, pious Jew, who would rather suffer than deny his nationality, that is most despised, but the modern Jew who, like the German outcasts in foreign countries, denies his nationality, while the hand of fate presses heavily upon his own people. The beautiful phrases about humanity and enlightenment which he employs as a cloak to hide his treason, his fear of being identified with his unfortunate brethren, will ultimately not protect him from the judgment of public opinion. In vain does the enlightened Jew hide behind his geographical and philosophical alibi. It is of no avail. Mask yourself a thousand times over, change your name, religion and character, travel throughout the world incognito, so that people may not recognize the Jew in you; yet every insult to the Jewish name will strike you, even more than the pious man who is permeated with the spirit of Jewish solidarity and who fights for the honor of the Jewish name.

Such, my friend, were my thoughts then, when I was actively engaged on behalf of the European Proletariat. My Messianic belief was, at that time, the same that I profess at present, namely, the belief in the regeneration of the historical civilized nations, which will be accomplished only by raising the oppressed nations to the level of the mighty and dominant ones. Now, as at the time I wrote my earlier works, I still believe that Christianity was a step forward on the road toward the goal of humanity, which the Jewish prophets termed the Messianic age. To-day, as ever, I still believe that the present great epoch in universal history had its first manifestation, at least in the history of the human spirit, in the teachings of Spinoza. However, I never believed, nor have I ever asserted, that Christianity is more than a mere episode in the sacred history of humanity, nor even that this epoch of sacredness closed with Spinoza. I have never doubted that we at present sigh and strive for a redemption which Christianity never dreamed of, nor could ever supply. It is true that Christianity shed a certain glow during the dark ages of history, after the sun of ancient civilization had set forever; but its light only revealed the graves of the nations of antiquity. Christianity is, after all, a religion of death, the function of which ceased the moment the nations reawakened into life. The history of the European nations for the last three hundred years amply illustrates the truth of this dictum; but I will restrict myself to calling your attention to the events transpiring at present in Italy. On the ruins of Christian Rome there rises the regenerated Italian people. An influence similar to that of Christianity is exerted by Islam in the East. Both religions teach resignation and submission, and Turkey follows the same policy in regard to Palestine that Austria exercises in Italy. Christianity and Islam are both only inscriptions on the tombstones which barbaric oppression erected upon the graves of weaker peoples. But the soldiers of civilization, the French, are gradually sweeping away the dominance of the barbarians and with their strong Herculean arms will roll off the tombstones from the graves of the supposedly dead peoples and the nations will reawaken once more.

In those countries which form a dividing line between the Occident and the Orient, namely, Russia, Poland, Prussia, Austria, and Turkey, there live millions of our brethren who earnestly believe in the restoration of the Jewish kingdom and pray for it fervently in their daily services. These Jews have preserved, by their belief in Jewish nationality, the very kernel of Judaism in a more faithful manner than have our Occidental Jews. The latter have endeavored to revive much of our religion, but not the great hope which created our faith and preserved it through all storms of time, namely, the hope of the restoration of Jewish nationality. To those millions of my brethren I turn and exclaim, "Carry thy standard high, oh my people!" The Jewish nation still preserves the fruitful seed of life, which, like the grains of corn found in the graves of Egyptian mummies, though buried for thousands of years, have never lost their power of productivity. The moment the rigid form in which it is enclosed is shattered, the seed, placed in the fertile soil of the present environment and given air and light, will strike root and prosper.

The rigid forms of orthodoxy, the existence of which was justified before the century of rebirth, will naturally, through the productive power of the national idea and the historical cult, relax and become fertile. It is only with the national rebirth that the religious genius of the Jews, like the giant of legend touching mother earth, will be endowed with new strength and again be reinspired with the prophetic spirit. No aspirant for enlightenment, not even a Mendelssohn, has so far succeeded in crushing the hard shell with which Rabbinism has encrusted Judaism without, at the same time, destroying the national ideal in its innermost essence.

SIXTH LETTER

The noble representatives of the German spirit—Patriotic Jews—The historian Graetz—Mercier's Essai sur la Litterature Juive—Autumn and Spring equinoxes of universal history and its storms—Sabbatai Zevi—Chasidim—Natural and historical religion—The Jewish Mother—Victor Hugo—Boerne, Baruch, Itzig.

You think my judgment in regard to the relation of the Germans to our brethren, as well as of the progressive German Jews to the Jewish people, too severe and dogmatic. You say that there are many noble spirits among the Germans who have banished from their hearts every trace of race prejudice and are permeated with the spirit of justice and humanity. And as for the progressive Jews, you think that many of them have always displayed a fine spirit of self-sacrifice when the honor of their religion or the welfare of their brethren called for it; and that those noble spirits came principally from the ranks of those who distinguished themselves in the field of science, or commerce, or industry, and thus acquired high positions in society. To these just strictures I willingly subscribe, for I admit that my judgment was too general in its character, and it can only be justified by the fact that it was written under the influence of the Damascus affair. To-day I would hesitate very much before subscribing to it. It cannot enter my mind, at present, to deny the Teutonic race, and especially the German people, whose mental power I esteem so highly, the ability to rise, by means of progress, above race prejudice. The German spirit has other representatives than patriotic Romanticists and philosophic book-dealers. A nation that produced men like Lessing, Herder, Schiller, Hegel, Humboldt and many more champions of humanity, must certainly possess the ability to rise to the heights of spirituality and idealism.

It occurs to me, in connection with what was said before, to relate a story, which will demonstrate the ability of the German spirit to overcome race prejudice. It was told to me by Ludwig Wihl. You have certainly heard of Hecker, who played such an important rôle in the political affairs of Baden in the forties, and even as late as the famous revolutionary year, 1848. A pure German of noblest birth, he began to attract attention in Baden by his much-heralded liberalism, immediately after the year of the Damascus affair. But do you know against which of the "hereditary enemies" this knight of German liberalism directed his attacks? Against the French, you will say? No, this hereditary enemy was rather harmless at the time, and under the leadership of Guizot and Louis Philippe. Was it against the Russians? Not against them. The hereditary enemy, in the attack against which Hecker won his spurs, was none other than the terrible and mighty people, the Jews. Hecker published a series of anonymous articles in the *Frankfurter Journal* against the emancipation of the Jews. A few years afterward it was this same Hecker who addressed a memorial, on behalf of Baden, to the Berlin Landtag of the Confederacy, favoring the emancipation of the Jews. And when people reproached him for his former opposition to the Jews, he openly confessed, that for a long time he had been unable to overcome his antipathy to the Jews, but that finally the principle of justice and humanity had triumphed in him.

The democrats of 1848 undoubtedly fully demonstrated their superiority over the demagogues of the "War of Liberation," the Romantic lads of the Jahn and Arndt type, whom they left far behind on the road of progress. And yet, on the basis of my long experience, I feel inclined to assert that Germany as a whole, in spite of its collective intellectuality, is in its practical social life far behind the rest of the civilized nations of Europe. The race war must first be fought out and definitely settled before social and humane ideas become part and parcel of the German people, as was the case with the Romance peoples which, after a long historical process, finally defeated race antagonism.

Willing as I am to correct my judgment in regard to German Anti-Semitism, I am still more willing to alter my former opinion, in accordance with your strictures, of our progressive Occidental Jews, and especially those of Germany. Of late there is to be observed in Judaism a wholesome spirit of reaction against the once dominating tendency of cosmopolitan philanthropy, that vague form of humanity which, as Jean Jacques Rousseau aptly remarked, professes to love men in general, so as not to be burdened with the immediate duties of benevolence to the individual. Signs of endeavor to introduce into Judaism a more healthy and natural spirit, I notice everywhere: in America, where new Jewish communities are founded and synagogues built every year; in France, where an attempt was made to found an *Alliance Israelite Universelle,* which may become an important factor in Jewish life, provided it be animated by a thorough Jewish national spirit; in the German and French literatures, where writers like Kompert, Strauben, Weill and Bernstein have portrayed Jewish life faithfully and beautifully, and with no small measure of success. But most of all is this tendency to regeneration prominent in the literature devoted to the science of Judaism, which, since the publication of the epoch-making History of the Jews, by Graetz, has developed such force that it will soon be able to overcome the nebulous Christianizing spiritualism of the assimilators.

Still earlier, Gabriel Riesser, one of our most progressive German Jews, had the courage to name his magazine, devoted to the interests of our political and civil rights, *The Jew.*[1] Dr. Ludwig Philipson, also, did not hesitate to call his spiritual child by the name *Israel.* Again, among the lyric poets, we have Ludwig Wihl who uses his muse to sing of the great memories of our immortal nation. It is certainly a sign of the times that Ludwig Wihl's *Westostliche Schwalben,* which for the last fifteen years hardly made any impression in Germany, was recently translated into French, with an introduction which attracted the attention of the French press to the Jewish people. Pierre Mercier, the French translator of the *Schwalben* in his *Essai sur la Litterature Juive,* an essay on Jewish Literature, expresses his opinion of this literature in a way which I cannot fully endorse. He views Judaism in the same way that Jesus did, namely, from the narrow and one-sided point of view of spiritualism. Yet his conception of the spirit that dominates the Torah is, in spite of its defects, vastly superior in its depth of historical understanding and broadness of sympathy with the Jewish genius, to those of the German historians who carry their Jew-hatred even to the Bible.

More interesting is his judgment of modern Jewish literature, which he considers an antidote against the modern decadent romantic literature. But he errs when he thinks that the wholesome source of this modern Jewish literature is Jewish spiritualization. Jewish life was never wholly spiritualized. Even the Essenes, who flourished among the Jews at the time of the birth of Christianity and to whom Christianity owes its origin, were not a thoroughly spiritualistic sect, and not even the primitive Christians can be considered as such. When the Essenic sect finally did become spiritualized through Christianity, it severed its relations with Judaism, and not even a trace of it can be found.[2] Almost every important point of departure in the history of the development of the great historical nations was accompanied by movements within that nation which is the bearer and creator of historical religion. The passing from antiquity into the Middle Ages, this autumn equinox of humanity, was heralded by great and stormy

[1] See Note IV at end of book.
[2] *Cf.,* on Jewish sects, Graetz, *History of the Jews,* Vol. III, note 10, German edition, and Vol. II in English. Luzzato, also expresses himself in connection with his remarks on Essenianism, decidedly against spiritualization and asceticism as being antagonistic to the spirit of Judaism. See his Commentary on Deut. vi, 5.

disturbances within Judaism which gave rise to Christianity, on the one hand, and to those sects within the pale of Judaism itself, on the other. But the sects were not of an enduring character; as soon as the crisis passed, they disappeared without leaving any traces behind. Also to-day, during the spring equinox of humanity, will the glorious future to which we strive be heralded by movements in Judaism. And although the world has not taken any cognizance of these stirrings in Judaism as yet, they are not therefore of less value than those that took place at the transition period from antiquity to the Middle Ages. Already at the beginning of the modern period, a Messianic movement, such as never occurred since the destruction of the Jewish State at the time of Bar Kochba, took hold of Eastern as well as Occidental Jews, a movement the false prophet of which was Sabbatai Zevi, but whose true prophet was Spinoza. Our modern Sadducees, Pharisees and Essenes, also I mean the reformers, the rabbinists and the Chasidim[3]—will disappear from Jewish history after the crisis has passed, the last crisis in universal history, when all the nations, and with them the Jewish people, will have awakened to a new life. Judaism does not allow either spiritualistic or materialistic sects to exist in its midst. Jewish life, like its divine ideal and goal, is undivided, and it is this Monism of Jewish life which acts as an antidote against modern materialism, which is only the reverse side of Christian spiritualism. I do not speak here of philosophical systems or of religious dogmas, or of life conceptions, but of life itself. Life is a product of the mental activity of the race, which forms its social institutions according to its inborn instincts and typical inclinations. Out of this primitive life-forming source springs later the life-view of a race, which in its turn influences life or rather modifies it, but is never able to alter essentially the primal type which continually reappears and takes the ascendancy.[4]

It was the German race that endowed the Christian world with the double aspect of spiritualism and materialism. The author of the *Essai sur la Litterature Juive* is right when he says that we are exceedingly generous in giving the entire credit for the modern love mania to Christianity. It is rather due to the Mediæval feeling of chivalry. The circumstances which produced this romantic sentimentality arose, not from the influence of Christianity alone, but from the combination of Christianity with old Germanic traditions. Without the contribution of the race genius of the Northern peoples, Christianity would have never occupied that position in universal history which it has occupied for centuries. Had it not been for those brave adventurers, the Teutonic knights of the Middle Ages, whose personal life oscillated between the two opposite poles of gross sensualism and the most abstract mysticism, Christian dualism would never have succeeded in impressing modern life so thoroughly and deeply. Thus it is not theory that forms life, but race; and likewise, it is not doctrine that made the Biblical-patriarchal life, which is the source of Jewish cult, but it is the patriarchal life of the Jewish ancestors that is the creative basis of the religion of the Bible, which is nothing else but a national historical cult developed out of family traditions.

Before the appearance of the Germanic races, there were only two forms of religion, the natural and the historical. The first found its typical expression in Greece, the second in Judæa. Just as the Greek cult had brought to light the perfection and charm of Nature, so Judaism revealed to us the force of the divine law in history. With the entrance of the Germanic race, both natural and historical religion lost their hold over the human mind and their influence was replaced by an apotheosis of the individual. Christianity found among the Northern races a natural inclination for that which in Christianity itself was only a result of the decay of the ancient nationalities, namely, that view of life which sees neither in Nature nor in history the unified divine life, but

[3]See Note V at end of book.
[4]Cf. Epilogue.

only the isolated existence of the individual.[5]

As long as the Germanic race dominates Europe, there can be no development of national life. The "religion of love," separated from natural and historical life, had only the salvation of the individual soul in view. The apotheosis of the individual terminated finally in a sentimental, feminine cult, which even to the present day possesses great attraction for our romantic Jews and inspires in them a sympathy for Christianity.

"Love," says Mercier, "was glorified and extolled, in all forms, as the noblest aim in life. The virtue of women, and even their vice, assumed an undue and all too important place in life, so that woman herself came to believe that the fate of the world depends upon her fidelity or infidelity. She therefore shared the fate of all those whom fortune has fondled too excessively, namely through undue flattery she became corrupted. And so it happened that love absorbed all social forces, all family tradition, and finally dissolved itself into sentimentality.

The Jews alone had the good sense to subordinate sexual to maternal love, Alexander Weill puts the following words in the mouth of a Jewish mother: "Should a true Jewish mother care for love? Love is a wicked form of idolatry. A Jewess must love only her God, her parents and her children..." The little old grandmother in Kompert's story says: "God cannot be present everywhere at the same time; He therefore created the mother..." Maternal love is represented in the Jewish novel as the basis of family life, as its passion and mystery. It is the same type of the Jewish mother which is repeated in all Jewish novels. There rises before me the picture of the Jewish mother, her face serene but pale, a melancholy smile plays around her lips and her deep, penetrating eye seems to gaze toward the distant future.

When you read these words of Mercier, you will certainly be reminded of your own mother, to whom this description aptly applies. There arose before me, also, on reading this description of the Jewish mother, the image of my own mother, whose features I still remember. I lost her in my youth at the age of fourteen, but till recently she appeared to me almost every night in my dreams, and I remember her words, as if they were uttered but yesterday, which she spoke to me when she visited me in Bonn. We were already in bed and had just finished the evening prayer. Then, speaking in an animated voice, she began: "Listen, my child, you must study diligently. Mohrich[6] was one of my ancestors, and you are fortunate that you are studying under your grandfather. It is written that 'when grandfather and grandchild study the Torah together, the study of the divine Law will never more forsake the family, but will be handed down from generation to generation.'"[7] The words of my mother must have impressed me deeply, for I still remember them distinctly, although I have never since heard nor read about the legend in regard to grandfather and grandchild.

Thus the thought of his children constitutes the central point around which the life and love of the Jew moves. Love is too strong an emotion in the Jewish heart, too Vast, to spend itself in sexual attraction and not embrace in its depth the generations of the future. And because of the fact that the eye of Jewish love is turned toward the future, the Jewish people has produced so many holy seers. A childless union is nowhere so much deplored as among the Jews. According to the rabbis, a childLess man is like unto the dead. Only the Jews could heartily join the great French poet,

[5]See Note VI at end of book.

[6]M'H'R'CH, the initials of one of the later rabbinical writers who fled from Poland into Germany so as to save his wife from the forced attentions of a Polish nobleman.—*Translator.*

[7]The words of my mother have their origin in a Talmudic saying (Baba Metziah, 85a) which utilizes the words of the verse, Ecclesiastes iv, 12: "And a threefold cord cannot be quickly broken,"

Victor Hugo, in his prayer:

Preserve my loved ones, Lord, I pray,
My kith and kin,—my enemies spare,
That never in the evil day
Our summers may of flowers be bare,
Our cages lacking trilling key,
Our honeycombs devoid of bee,
Or childless house to ever see.

I close with the above verses cited by Mercier, a subject which we discussed at some length,[8] but in the interests of the national regeneration of our people, it must be constantly emphasized. If it is gratifying to see that inspired poets and writers champion the cause of our nationality, it is still more fortunate that the loyalty to a people, with whose help the oppressed nation will reawaken, was not unknown among the Jews. What would this people, I mean the French, think of us, when during the springtime of nations, the daybreak of the French Revolution, not a sound of loyalty and sympathy was heard in the midst of our nation? But thanks to the French translator of the *Schwalben*, the stain was removed from our name. Although neither Wihl nor the other Jewish writers and poets have expressed themselves for our own political regeneration, they have, at least, shown to the world that progressive Judaism also cherishes patriotic memories, and that through some stimulus this poetic and ideal patriotism may be converted into a strong and mighty force of action. And, therefore, I do not doubt, that from now on, progressive Jews will labor for the political regeneration of our people with the same energy that other Jews, in other times, have labored for the emancipation of the Jews in the lands of exile. The springtime of nations which is about to merge into the fruit-ripening Summer, will not pass without leaving a lasting impression upon our Occidental brethren. Among the Jews, also, Spring will quietly fructify the buds, and the bloom of a new life will suddenly surprise every beholder. The young Jewish generation, sensitive to every high and noble ideal, will enthusiastically join the Jewish national movement; and once the young branch turns its growing force in that direction, even the barren trunk will soon be covered with leaves and flowers that will be an ornament to Israel.

Till now, however, beloved friend, the barren wood preponderates in Occidental Judaism. Most of the German Jews, as soon as they come in contact with European civilization, begin to feel ashamed of their religion and descent. The Germans have so frequently and thoroughly demonstrated to us that our nationality is an obstacle to our "inner" emancipation, that we have finally come to believe it ourselves and, giving up our Jewish culture and denying our race, have made every effort to be deserving of the "blond" Germanism. Yet in spite of the excellent mathematicians among them, our Jewish Teutomaniacs, who bartered away their Judaism for State positions, grossly miscalculated their chances. It did not avail Meyerbeer that he painstakingly avoided the use of a Jewish theme as the subject of any of his operas; he did not escape, on that account, the hatred of the Germans. The old honest *Augsburger Allgemeine Zeitung* seldom refrained, while mentioning his name, from remarking parenthetically, "Jacob Meyer Lippman Beer." The German patriot Boerne, likewise, did not gain much by changing his family name, Baruch, into that of Boerne. He admits it himself. "Whenever my enemies founder upon the rock of Börne," he writes, "they throw out, as an anchor of safety, the name Baruch." I have experienced it personally, not only with opponents, but even with my own party members. In personal controversy they always make use of the "Hep" weapon, and in Germany it is always effective. I have

---

[8]Hess refers to the translation of the "Schwalben" poems by Wihl which he discussed at length and which seem to express a certain amount of enthusiasm for the French people.—*Translator*.

made it easy for them to wield their weapon by adopting my Old Testament name Moses. I regret exceedingly that my name is not Itzig.

SEVENTH LETTER

The Reform trick and the uncritical reaction—Luther and Mendelssohn—The rationalistic double—The key to the religion of the future—The three epochs in the development of the Jewish spirit—Restoration of the Jewish State.

The question you asked me, the answer to which constitutes the most difficult problem of Nineteenth Century Jewry, shows me that you have finally begun to interest yourself in Jewish affairs. You have, then, nothing against the attempt to raise the Jews once more to their former place in universal history. But you believe that this aspiration is merely a desire, and that at the present time, world Jewry consists only of a number of scattered and dispersed Jewish families, but is not a nation. The religious tie, which till now has bound the scattered members together and united them into a single entity, is now severed through the participation of Jews in the general cultural life. True, the reformers have tried to mend the situation, but they have succeeded only in widening the breach. And with barren orthodoxy and the uncritical reactionaries—those who still believe that the Polish fur cap is a law given orally to Moses on Sinai and handed down by the sages—it is useless to argue.

The inevitable result of this situation is, you think, indifference and severance from Judaism. Nobody can be held responsible for this precarious situation, for it is not the arbitrariness of man, but the force of circumstances that has dissolved the unity of orthodox Judaism. Which community, you ask, which synagogue, shall one who is still attached to his people, join? Again, you call out maliciously, shall we condemn our Jewish scholars for their attempt to give us, in lieu of the "externally shattered" hard shell of Rabbinism, the light of Science?

No, my dear friend, we will not hold anyone responsible for a crisis, though a dangerous one, but one which is, after all, wholesome and necessary. No human power could have avoided it, but its gravest symptoms are gradually disappearing and we have no fear of its repetition. Judaism, which in its first contact with modern civilization was threatened with dissolution—we say it without fear of being contradicted by history—has successfully withstood this last danger, perhaps the greatest that ever threatened its existence. Judaism, at present, expect no antagonism either from science or from life, but only from those who pose as its representatives without having the right to do so.

Far be it from me to minimize the untiring labor of the Jewish scholars to whom our present Jewish generation owes its education, social position, and mental and moral progress, and whom alone we have to thank for the fact that in the midst of an almost universal social disintegration the Jewish family still serves as a model of moral conduct. These scholars and teachers are the successors of the ancient rabbis, who were the support and stay of Judaism during the long two thousand year exile, and who, nevertheless, never formed themselves into a caste.

Yet even they, like our poets, are so much engrossed by the general current of life, that they hardly devote any time to thought about our national regeneration. And as with the Jewish scholars, so is it with the young generation; they need some external stimulus to rouse their dormant national feelings, so that they will proclaim themselves openly as Jewish patriots. The threatening danger to Judaism comes only from the religious reformers who, with their newly-invented ceremonies and empty eloquence nave sucked the marrow out of Judaism and left only its skeleton. It was not enough for them to aspire to spread and develop Jewish study on scientific principles, nor were they satisfied with a regulated, æsthetic form of our ancient Jewish cult. Their religious reform was inopportunely borrowed from a foreign religious denomination, and has no basis or justification either in the conditions of the modern world or in the essential teachings of national Judaism. I do not deny the justification of the Christian Reformation at the time of Luther, nor of the Jewish reform movement at the time of Mendelssohn. The latter, however, was more of an æsthetic than a religious or scientific reform. Those reformers keenly appreciated the historical basis of a religion and knew well that the old basis cannot be arbitrarily replaced by a new one. Our reformers, on the contrary, attempted to reform the basis itself. Their reforms have only a negative purpose—if they have any aim at all—to firmly establish unbelief in the national foundation of the Jewish religion. No wonder that these reforms only fostered indifference to Judaism and conversions to Christianity. Judaism, like Christianity, would have to disappear as a result of the general state of enlightenment and progress, if it were not more than a mere dogmatic religion, namely, a national cult. The Jewish reformers, however, those who are still present in some German communities, and maintain, to the best of their ability, the theatrical show of religious reform, know so little of the value of national Judaism, that they are at great pains to erase carefully from their creed and worship all traces of Jewish nationalism. They fancy that a recently manufactured prayer or hymn book, wherein a philosophical theism is put into rhyme and accompanied by music, is more elevating and soul-stirring than the fervent Hebrew prayers which express the pain and sorrow of a nation at the loss of its fatherland. They forget that these prayers, which not only created, but preserved for millenniums, the unity of Jewish worship, are even to-day the tie which binds into one people all the Jews scattered around the globe.[1]

The efforts of our German Jewish religious reformers tended to the conversion of our national and humanitarian Judaism into a second Christianity cut after a rationalistic pattern, at a time when Christianity itself was already in a state of disintegration. Christianity, which came into existence on the graves of the ancient nations, had to withdraw from participation in national life. It therefore must continue to suffer from internal dissensions arising from the constant clash of irreconcilable principles, until it is finally replaced among the regenerated nations by a new historical cult. To this coming cult, Judaism alone holds the key. This "religion of the future" of which the eighteenth century philosophers, as well as their recent followers, dreamed, will neither be an imitation of the ancient pagan Nature cult, nor a reflection of the neo-Christian or the neo-Judaism skeleton, the specter of which haunts the minds of our religious reformers. Each nation will have to create its own historical cult; each people must become like the Jewish people, a people of God.

Judaism is not threatened, like Christianity, with danger from the nationalistic and humanistic aspirations of our time, for in reality, these sentiments belong to the very essence of Judaism. It is a very prevalent error, most likely borrowed from Christianity, that an entire view of life can be compressed into a single dogma. I do not agree with Mendelssohn that Judaism has no dogmas. I claim that the divine teaching of Judaism was never, at any time, completed and finished. It has always kept on developing, its development being based upon the harmonizing of the Jewish genius with that of life and humanity. Development of the knowledge of God, through study and conscientious investigation, is not only not forbidden in Judaism, but is even considered a religious duty. This is the reason why Judaism never excluded

[1]If the reformers cannot entirely supplant the prayers by hymns, they attempt, at least, to amend them. Dr. Hirsch, Rabbi of Luxemburg, changed the expression "who restorest thy divine presence unto Zion," in the Eighteen Benedictions, to "whom alone we serve in reverence." Some reformers are satisfied to omit from the Prayer Book the beautiful hymn Yigdal, for the reason that the belief in the Messianic age is poetically expressed in this song. It seems that the reformers think that the Messianic belief, which is the soul of Judaism, found its expression only in these few prayers and poems, and they cannot conceive that it is the underlying basis of the whole Jewish Cult.

philosophical thought or even condemned it, and also why it has never occurred to any good Jew to "reform" Judaism according to his philosophical conceptions. Hence there were no real sects in Judaism. Even recently, when there was no lack of orthodox and heterodox dogmatists in Jewry, there arose no sects; for the dogmatic basis of Judaism is so wide, that it allows free play to every mental speculation and creation. Differences of opinion in regard to metaphysical conceptions have always obtained among the Jews, but Judaism has never excluded anyone. The apostates *severed themselves* from the bond of Jewry. "And not even them has Judaism forsaken," added a learned rabbi, in whose presence I expressed the above quoted opinion.

In reality, Judaism as a nationality has a natural basis which cannot be set aside by mere conversion to another faith, as is the case in other religions. A Jew belongs to his race and consequently also to Judaism, in spite of the fact that he or his ancestors have become apostates. It may appear paradoxical, according to our modern religious opinions, but in life, at least, I have observed this view to be true. The converted Jew remains a Jew no matter how much he objects to it. At present, there is but little difference between the enlightened and the converted Jew. My friend, Armond L——, whose grandfather had already been converted, is more interested in Jewish affairs than many a circumcised Jew, and he has preserved his faith in Jewish nationality more faithfully than our enlightened rabbis.

The Jew was not commanded to believe, but to search after the knowledge of God. Belief is a matter of conscience, for which we are not accountable to anyone but ourselves. It is impossible to give it to another. It is very easy, indeed, for false rationalism, just as for blind faith, to drawl forth its creed. But real religion, which grows out of the innermost life of the soul, develops with the individual. Humanity cannot be formulated completely and embraced in a set of articles of creed. On the wide, dogmatic basis of Judaism, many and various views of life were able to develop. But for creative Judaism itself, these various views of life were only passing phases, the result of internal and external experiences; and in spite of this multiplicity of forms of development, the original type never disappeared, but was constantly reproduced as the ripe fruit of the tree of life.

The noble Jewish spirits and the great thinkers of Israel understood this peculiar character of historical Judaism. They did see in every modification of the view of life a new religion, and never persuaded themselves that they could reform the historical basis of our religion. Saadia and Maimonides, Spinoza and Mendelssohn did not become apostates, in spite of their progressive spirit, though there were many fanatics who wanted to exclude them from Judaism, or, as in the case of Spinoza, had him excluded. Our modern rationalists would excommunicate from the Synagogue Jews who declare themselves Spinozists, if they only had the power.

Dissatisfied with reform and repulsed by the fanaticism of the orthodox and heterodox, you ask me, with which religious faction should one affiliate with his family in these days? I know only one religious fellowship, the old Synagogue, which is fortunately still in existence and will, I hope, exist until the national regeneration of world Jewry is accomplished. I myself, had I a family, would, in spite of my dogmatic heterodoxy, not only join an orthodox synagogue, but would also observe in my house all feast and fast days, so as to keep alive in my heart and in the heart of my children, the traditions of my people. If I had influence in the synagogue, I would endeavor to beautify the religious worship. Above all, I would see to it that scholarly Jewish teachers and preachers should assume their proper positions and be reverently respected. I would then turn my hand to other reforms, if you care to call them such, but of a different kind than those spiritless and empty reforms favored by our religious reformers. No ancient custom or usage should be changed, no Hebrew prayer should be shortened or read in German translation. And, finally, no Sabbath or Festival should be abolished or be postponed to the Christian day of rest. The *Hazan* and singers should not be mere soulless singing machines. The prayers and hymns should be read and sung by pious men and boys, who are not only versed in music, but also in religious matters. The house of prayer is not a theater and the cantor and singers, as well as the preacher, should be something more than mere comedians. What does not come from the heart can never affect the heart. Prayers, songs and sermons, which treat our holy national worship as an antiquated institution, cannot exalt the soul; they always arouse in me an unconquerable aversion. In a word, I would favor everything which would contribute to the elevation and education of the congregation, without, at the same time, undermining our ancient worship. And in my own family circle, also, I would carefully see that the traditions of our people are strictly observed.

If people were to follow the policy outlined above, peace would reign in Jewish communities, and the religious cravings of every Jew, no matter what view of life he holds, would be better satisfied than they are with the reforms that every intellectual bungler fashions after his own individual pattern. These unsystematic reforms only terminate in a meaningless nihilism, which brings in its train desolation of spirit and a continual estrangement from Judaism on the part of our young generation.

We really confer too much honor upon reform when we call it a free, intellectual movement, in the higher sense. True, in a negative sense, we may call rationalistic criticism a free tendency, for the negation of antiquated principles is the first step toward freedom. But positive freedom is an autonomous development, and when rationalistic reform denies the essence of Judaism, namely, its nationalism, it cannot become a creative factor, and consequently cannot be said to be free in the higher sense. Its services on behalf of negative criticism are very slight; and these, as you rightly remarked, are for the most part, due to the circumstances and conditions of a revolutionary age for which the reformers can hardly be held responsible.

Modern social life, the outcome of the revolution, is regenerating in its nature; it does not occupy itself solely with tearing down the old, but is mainly busy with creating new forms. At the basis of every creation, however, there is something of the old, for *ex nihilo nihil*, out of nothing, nothing can be created. The national-humanitarian essence of the Jewish historical religion is the germ out of which future social creations will spring forth. As long as Jews misconceive the essence of the spirit of modern times, which was originally their own spirit, they will only be dragged along involuntarily by the current of modern history, but will not participate in its making. In order to be influenced by modern life, there was no necessity for rationalistic reform. Such countries as the Rhine provinces and France clearly demonstrate this. In these countries the current of modern life is at its height, yet rationalistic, religious reform has hardly appeared there. It is in these countries, too, that religious indifference has been brought about without the help of a reform movement. Even orthodox Jewry itself, in modern Europe, is gradually being carried away by the current, as can be seen by the fact that the most important function of Rabbinism, namely, its jurisdiction, has disappeared, without the slightest protest on the part of orthodoxy.[2] Reform has only gone a step further—to raise this groundless negation to the rank of a principle, or, as remarked above, has sanctioned unbelief. We could well afford not to begrudge the reformers their laurels, had they not persuaded themselves

---

[2]Hess refers to the rabbinical courts and the jurisdiction they had exercised in civil cases between Jew and Jew. The power of these courts in Western Jewish communities began to decline as early as the beginning of the 19th Century, and was completely abrogated by the middle of the century. In Russia and other parts of Eastern Jewry, the Rabbinic courts are still maintained in most Jewish communities.—*Translator.*

that they had created something positive. Imitating Christian reformers of an earlier age, they set up the Bible, in contradistinction to the Talmud, as the positive content of regenerated Judaism, and by this anachronism, which was merely an imitation of a foreign movement, they only made themselves ridiculous. It is, in reality, a narrower point of view than that of orthodox Judaism, to declare the living, oral tradition to be a "human fiction," and because it was written down at a later time, to discard it, while admitting the law of the Bible to be divine. This view is also unhistorical. Everything tends to show that until the Babylonian exile, or even still later, until the period of the *Sopherim,* no distinction was made between the written and the oral laws, as is the case to-day. It is only after the time of the *Sopherim* that this distinction was made. Until then, tradition was neither exclusively written nor exclusively oral. How this separation was effected has not yet been clearly demonstrated by critical historians. But one thing is firmly established, namely, that the spirit which at the time of the restoration inspired the *Sopherim* and the sages of the Great Synagogue, was freer, holier, and more patriotic, than the spirit which inspired Moses and the Prophets. Every liberation from a politico-social slavery is at the same time a liberation of the spirit and serves as a means of fertilizing the national genius.

There are two epochs that mark the development of Jewish law: the first, after the liberation from Egypt; the second, after the return from Babylonia. The third is yet to come, with the redemption from the third exile. The significance of the second legislative epoch is more misunderstood by our reformers (who have no conception of the creative genius of the Jewish nation), than by our rabbis, who place the law-givers of this period even higher than Moses, for they say: "Ezra would have deserved that the Torah be given to Israel through him, had not Moses preceded him." In the form in which we possess it to-day, the Torah was handed down to us directly through the men of that epoch. These same men, living at the same time, utilizing the same traditions, and in the same spirit, collected both the written and the oral law, which they handed down to later generations. Nothing entitles the written law to a holier origin than the oral. On the contrary, the free development of the law by oral tradition, from the time of the return from the Babylonian exile, was always considered of greater importance than the mere clinging to the written law. The reason for this is quite evident. The national legislative genius would have been extinguished, had the sages not occupied themselves with the living development of the law. It was to this occupation that Judaism owed its national renaissance after the Babylonian exile, as well as its existence in the Diaspora. It was through this, that the great heroes who fought so bravely against the Greeks and Romans, rose in Israel. And, finally, it is to this oral development of the law that Judaism owes its existence during the two thousand years of exile; and to it the Jewish people will also owe its future national regeneration.

The rabbis were justified in their long struggle against writing down the oral law. Had they kept on teaching and developing the law orally in the schools, Judaism would never have been threatened with the loss of its national legislative genius. But they were compelled to reduce the law to writing, in order to avoid a still greater danger, namely, its being entirely forgotten, especially in the Diaspora. To-day, we have no reason to fear the latter danger. But we can escape the former, only if we set up the spirit of criticism against barren formalism and dissolving rationalism and revive in our hearts and souls the holy, patriotic spirit of our prophets and sages. We have to restudy our history, which has been grossly neglected by our rationalists, and rekindle in the hearts of our young generation the spirit which was the source of inspiration to our prophets and sages. Then, also, will we draw our inspiration from the deep well of Judaism; then will our sages and wise men regain the authority which they forfeited

47

from the moment when, prompted by other motives than patriotism, they estranged themselves from Judaism and attempted to reform the Jewish law. We will then again become participators in the holy spirit, namely, the Jewish genius, which alone has the right to develop and form the Jewish law according to the needs of the people. And then, when the third exile will finally have come to an end, the restoration of the Jewish State will find us ready for it.

Eighth Letter

The Neo-Hebraic literature—Luzzato, Rappoport, Frankel, Krochmal, Sachs and Heine on Judah Halevi— Mendelssohn and the Modernists—Schorr—Sectarians without sects— Salvador—Fusionists and Freemasons—Hirsch—The pretended calling of the Jew in exile.

You are certainly in error, dear friend, when you believe that only our progressive Jews have acquired the mastery of modern culture and science and that orthodox Jews are still steeped in Egyptian darkness, a condition which is as detrimental to the renaissance of our nation as is modern indifference. Since I have devoted myself to the cause of my people, I have, partly through personal contact and partly through their writings, come to know many orthodox Jews of the old as well as of the younger generation and especially of the latter, who do not fall behind the enlightened Jews, in scientific and literary education. These scholars have, at the same time, a more thorough understanding and conception of the past as well as of the future, than those enlightened minds who lack the philosophic and historical sense.

Orthodox Jewry everywhere, in England, France, Italy, Germany, Hungary, Poland and Bohemia, has its literary and scientific representatives who are as worthy as those of enlightened Jewry. Newspapers, magazines and even philosophical books, permeated with the same spirit of true humanitarianism as the nation to which they belong, are published by our orthodox brethren in the sacred tongue of their fathers. Hebrew literature, thanks to the works of Luzzato, Rappoport, Frankel and Krochmal, was reawakened to new life, and already a number of educated modern German rabbis conduct their correspondence in Hebrew. Even Holdheim himself did not disdain to compose his swan song in Hebrew; and Schorr, a more violent opponent of orthodoxy than Holdheim publishes his periodical *Hachalutz* in Hebrew. How great must the influence exerted by National Judaism be, when even its opponents are forced to employ its own medium in order to gain a hearing.

Read the work of Dr. Sachs, *The Religious Poetry of the Spanish Jews.* This book, written in the finest style, will convince you that educated orthodox Jews exert a far more wholesome influence on Judaism than the reformers. The last only reflect, on the ruins of a fossilized orthodoxy, a cold, borrowed light of a by-gone epoch, without possessing either the light or the warmth of new life themselves. You perhaps know, from reading Heine's *Romancero,* the tragic end of this great patriot and sacred singer, Judah Halevi who, according to the legend, met his death at the ruins of the Temple at Jerusalem, whither he was driven by his irresistible longing to visit the land of his fathers. You will certainly be interested to learn a few things about the life and character of this pious bard who enriched our prayer book with his beautiful and noble poems. "The one," says Dr. Sachs, "who cannot theoretically conceive the solution of the problem, how a dispersed people may possess a nationality and a homeless nation a fatherland, will find in the personality of this great singer and in his poetry, a practical solution to that problem." I must here remark that the Judæo-Spanish cultural epoch succeeded in solving one more grave problem, namely, how it is possible to be a good, patriotic, national Jew, in the full sense of the word, and at the same time participate in the cultural and political life of the land to such a degree that the land may become a second fatherland. "The longing for the hour of redemption," continues Sachs, "is the dominant note in the Jewish poetry of the Spanish period. With many, it was the oppressive conditions of existence that called forth that irrepressible longing. But with Halevi, this longing is a pure, loving desire, which possesses, on the one hand, the simplicity and naivete of childhood and; on the other, the glow of a mighty passion. The energy and vividness with which he expresses his confidence in the redemption of his people is only the more gripping, because of the fact that in his poetry there is no trace of the gloomy present, and his hope of the future does not appear to be the result of a daring escape from the dark environment which surrounds him, into the shining regions of phantasy. He is confident of his cause and the joy of his belief intoxicates and inspires him."

This confidence and joy of belief remind me vividly of my pious grandfather. Whenever they spoke to him of plans for the future, he always objected to making such plans, remarking that we Jews, being in exile, have no right to plan for the future, as—the Messiah may suddenly arrive. My grandfather was neither a poet nor a prophet; he was only a plain business man, who in the daytime attended to his routine work, that he might support his family and in the night devoted himself to religious and scholarly studies. After the dispersion, study became, as you can find again in Sachs, an essential and inseparable part of the national cult. "The house of study," he says, "became the only central point of an independent, free life, and the teachers were the bearers of all ideals which were typical and characteristic of national Judaism." The Synagogue was rather a schoolhouse than a house of prayer. Even to the present day, it is still designed, by the German Jews, as "Schul." The typical national cult, finding its expression in the study and in the minute observance of thousands of precepts with which Judaism fenced itself around in order to preserve its integrity in dispersion, is misconceived by our enlightened Jews. These legal and religious precepts and commandments, which permeate the whole life of the Jew, are condemned and mocked at by blockheads, who have not the least conception of the patriotic significance of these precepts and who consider themselves progressive only because they have turned their back on the traditions of their people. It is the same tendency which came to the front immediately after the appearance of Mendelssohn and which caused Mendelssohn himself pain and aggravation. During the life of Mendelssohn, there emerged those "Modern Jews" who measure the degree of enlightenment and education one possesses by the amount of his disregard for Jewish customs, and who finally graduated into State service by presenting a conversion certificate as their diploma. They relate an anecdote which originated during that first epoch of Jewish enlightenment and which is characteristic of that period. A Jew came to Mendelssohn and boasted of his son's philosophical ability. When the great Berlin philosopher asked the father wherein the philosophical acumen of his son consisted, the happy man replied, "Why my son has not put on his *tephillin* for months."

You know that the use of phylacteries on the forehead and the hand originates in a Mosaic command. It is prescribed in the Pentateuch, that in order to remember the divine teaching, we should inscribe the words of God's law on the doorposts of our houses, and symbolize that teaching by wearing fringes on our garments, binding the phylacteries "as a sign upon the arm and as frontlets between the eyes." We find pictures of garments with such fringes on the old Egyptian monuments, which proves that this custom is a very ancient one. But even assuming with Schorr that the custom of putting on phylacteries is not as old as that of wearing fringes on the garments, the results of Schorr's investigation were not known to that "enlightened" son and his happy father; just as they were unknown to the Berlin philosopher, who conscientiously put on his *tephillin* every day and observed all the Jewish customs. The enlightened *epikoros* could by no means understand Mendelssohn's conscientious attachment to traditional Judaism. His relation to orthodox Judaism was not, as Mendelssohn persuaded himself, a logical result of his rationalism, but was a natural expression of his true Jewish spirit. His fine sense of religiosity told him, that when a man turns his back on tradition, he really severs himself from Judaism itself and from its national essence. It is one thing to restore Judaism, through unbiased historical criticism, to its origins; it is quite another to discard it and belittle it through indifference and imitation. You, who declare the teachings and ordinances of our sages to be foolish inventions, pray to tell us what would have become of Judaism and the Jews if they had not, through the institutions of the Talmudic sages, thrown a protecting fence around their religion, so as to safeguard it for the coming days? Would they have continued to exist for eighteen hundred years and have resisted the influence of Christian and Mohammedan civilization? Would they not long ago have disappeared as a nation from the face of the earth, had they not, after they were driven out of their own land, created out of the confines of their own life, a sacred territory for their existence and a soil on which they could thrive?

To those who lack the historical sense, the existence of one nation more or less is of little importance for the historical development of humanity. The great organic creation of Jewish literature which, for the last three thousand years, was a gradual growth out of the national essence of Judaism, seems to the spiritual dwarfs, the rationalist, to be no more than an unnecessary growth which, even in our age of enlightenment, has not been sufficiently eradicated. These pygmies, who are living in an age of giants, do not realize that their very existence is an anachronism. As a precursor of the French Revolution, in the century of *The Critique of Pure Reason,* the existence of rationalism was justified. But to-day, when the shackles of dogmatism have long been shaken off, we feel more the need of creating new values, and for this purpose utilize the creations of all ages, than the continuation of mere negative criticism which has, at present, but little value for us. The desire to create new values is felt even by those who are unable to discern the creative ability in the expressions of the Jewish spirit, and are thus unable to utilize the previous creations of Judaism as a basis. But in their ignorance and mental helplessness, they turned, in their desire for creation, to external, artificial means, which do not spring from the deep well of our people's life.

In Jewry, as well as in the entire modern world, there are to be discovered at present, two main tendencies which, though diametrically opposed to each other, still originate from the same course, namely, the need of objective religious norms and the inability to create them. One tendency, as a result of the above-mentioned cause, expresses itself on the part of some people in turning back to the old uncritical belief which, however, with them, lost its naive and true character. In their despair, which arose as a result of the dominant nihilism, they insist on a conscious contradiction to all reason. This desperate reaction, which defies the results of criticism and spiritual revolution, is known in the Christian world as Supernaturalism. In the Jewish world, it is represented by Hirsch, of Frankfort A/M, and other less gifted spirits, as well as by a host of ignoramuses and hypocrites, whose association with it really lessens its dignity. As an antidote against this reaction, the negative reform aspirations may possess some justification, even though, from the point of view of reason, they did not succeed in creating any stable solid life norms. The characteristic trait of the negative spiritual tendency, which labored in vain to create something of a general Jewish value, is its extreme individualism and incoherence. The modern religious reformers are sectarians without sects. Each of our Jewish Protestants has his own code. Out of this chaos of opinions there will undoubtedly in time develop a new Jewish life. But this new life, the beginnings of which are already noticeable in the activities of the younger generation of Jewish scholars, will bring entirely different results from those hitherto expected in the liberal circles of German Jewry.

French Jewry, also, within which there is not as yet, and perhaps there never will be, any cleavage on the lines of reform and orthodoxy, is not free from the traces of a tendency which strives after a fusion of all historical cults into one, and which endeavors to reach its aim by removing from the various religions their historical and characteristic traits, retaining only their common elements. You have certainly heard of Joseph Salvador, the author of the work entitled *History of the Mosaic Institutions and of the Hebrew People.* This same author recently published a work entitled *Paris, Rome and Jerusalem,* in which he clearly shows that even among our enlightened brethren, there are dreamers who wish for a rebuilding of the Temple of Jerusalem. But he attaches to this rebuilding conditions that are acceptable neither to pious nor to progressive Christians and Jews. If I understand the author correctly, he expects his New Jerusalem to become the world capital of the fusionists. Salvador, furthermore, seems to cherish the curious idea that the Jews ought first to turn Christians, so that they may be the better able to convert the Christians afterward to Judaism. This work is, in reality, not as new as Salvador thinks; it began eighteen hundred years ago. It seems, however, that the Judaism of which Salvador is thinking is as new as his Christianity.

More reasonable are the attempts of those fusionists who, like my friend Hirsch, of Luxemburg, are utilizing freemasonry as a means to amalgamate all the historical cults into one. The Luxemburg Rabbi, the antipode of his namesake, the Frankfort Rabbi Hirsch, developed the idea of fusion so thoroughly in the excellent lectures which he delivered at the Luxemburg Lodge, and later published under the title *Humanity as a Religion*, that, according to him, the matter may be considered closed, All that remains for the rabbis to do is to close up their reform temples and send the school children to the Masonic temples. In truth, the logical consequences of reform have long since led those who took the sermons of the reform rabbis seriously, toward making such a step; as you, being a resident of Frankfort, well know. In vain did they afterward ornament their fusionist sermons with Talmudic quotations. It was too late and they had to be satisfied to preach to empty pews.

Jewish rationalists, who have as little reason to remain within the fold of Judaism as have Christian rationalists for clinging to Christianity are, like their Christian friends, very energetic in discovering new grounds for the existence of a religion which, according to them, has no longer any reason to exist. According to them, the dispersion of the Jews was merely a preliminary step to their entering upon their great mission. What great things are the Jews in exile to accomplish in their opinion? First of all, they are to represent "pure" theism, in contradistinction to Christianity. In the next place, tolerant Judaism is to teach intolerant Christianity the principles of humanitarianism. Furthermore, it is the function of exilic Judaism to take care that morality and life, which in the Christian world are severed from each other, should become one. And lastly, the Jews must also act as industrial and commercial promoters —be the leaven of such activities among the civilized nations in whose midst they live. I have even heard it remarked quite seriously, that the Indo-Germanic race must improve its quality by mingling with the Jewish race!

But, mark you, from all these real or imaginary benefits which the Jews in dispersion confer upon the world, none will be diminished even after the restoration of the Jewish State. For just as at the time of the return from the Babylonian exile not all the Jews settled in Palestine, but the majority remained in the lands of exile, where there had been Jewish settlements since the dispersion of Israel and Judah, so need we not look forward to a larger concentration of Jews at the future restoration. Besides, it seems to me that those benefits which the Jews in exile confer upon the world are exaggerated, "for the sake of the cause." I consider it an anachronism to assign to the Jews those missions which they certainly performed in antiquity, and to some extent also in Mediæval times, but which, at present, no longer belong peculiarly to them. As to affecting the unity of life and theory, it is only possible with a nation which is politically organized; such a nation alone is able to realize it practically by embodying it in its institutions.

Again, what section of world. Jewry is to teach the Christians tolerance and humanity? You will surely say the enlightened Jews. But is not the enlightened Christian entitled to repeat to the enlightened Jew the words which Lessing, in his *Nathan the Wise*, puts into the mouth of the liberal Christian in his answer to the liberal Jew: "What makes me a Christian in your eyes, makes you a Jew in mine."

Or, on the other hand, should the enlightened Jew say to the orthodox Christian, "Your beliefs are mere superstitions, your religion only fanaticism," may the enlightened Christian not turn to the orthodox Jew and make similar remarks in defense of his own religion? Our cultured Jews who accuse Christians of possessing a persecution mania, reason as fallaciously as does Bethmann Hollweg when he charges the Jews with the same trait. History can neither be explained nor changed in its course by such explanations.

From the viewpoint of enlightenment, I see as little reason for the continuation of the existence of Judaism as for Christianity. It is better for the Jew who does not believe in the national regeneration of his people, to labor, like the enlightened Christian, for the dissolution of his religion. I understand how one can hold such an opinion. But what I do not understand is, how it is possible to believe simultaneously in "enlightenment" and in a Jewish Mission in exile; in other words, in the ultimate dissolution and in the continued existence of Judaism at the same time.

NINTH LETTER

A dilemma—The sacred history of mankind—Our allies—The unity of the human genus —Races and folk types—The organism of mankind.

You confronted me with the dilemma, that we must either agree with the Luxemburg Hirsch, that the goal and essence of Judaism is humanitarianism, in which case it is not national regeneration, but the realization of humanitarian ideals which is the aim worth striving for;—and Judaism, like every religious or political society; must ultimately become absorbed and disappear in the larger fellowship of humanity;—or we must agree with the Frankfort Hirsch, who sees in Judaism the only salvation; in which case, we disagree with the modern humanitarian aspirations and, like orthodox Christianity, we need make little appeal to public opinion of the century; for public opinion will receive such an appeal with the same feeling that it would receive a Chinese Proclamation or a Papal Bull.

I believe, dear friend that the opinions I have heretofore expressed in my correspondence with you have little in common with either horn of the dilemma. They do not agree with the conceptions of either extreme faction, but belong to a different order of ideas; I believe that not only does the national essence of Judaism not exclude civilization and humanitarianism, but that the latter really follow from it, as necessarily as the result follows from the cause. If, in spite of this, I emphasize the national side of Judaism, which is the root, rather than the humanitarian aspect, which is the bloom and flower, it is because in our time people are prone to decorate themselves with the flowers of culture rather than cultivate them again in the soil on which they grew. It is out of Judaism that our humanitarian view of life sprang. There is not a phase in Christian morality, nor in the scholastic philosophy of the Middle Ages,[1] nor in modern philanthropy, and, if we add the latest manifestation of Judaism, Spinozism, not even in modern philosophy, which does not have its roots in Judaism. Until the French Revolution, the Jewish people was the only people in the world which had, simultaneously, a national as well as a humanitarian religion. It is through Judaism that the history of humanity became a sacred history. I mean by that, that process of unified organic development which has its origin in the love of the family and which will not be completed until the whole of humanity becomes one family, the members of which will be united by the holy spirit, the creative genius of history, as strongly as the organs of a body are united by the creative natural forces. As long as no other people possessed such a national, humanitarian cult, the Jews alone were the people of God. Since the French Revolution, the French, as well as the other peoples which followed them, have become our noble rivals and faithful allies.

With the final victory of these nations over Mediæval reaction, the humanitarian aspirations, with which I am greatly in sympathy, so long as they do not express themselves merely in hypocritical, flowery words, will be realized and bear fruit. Anti-

---

[1]Munk, in his *Mélanges de philosophie juive et arabe*, pp. 291-301, has already shown the influence of Avicebron on Scholastic philosophy. The *Mekor Hayim* (Source of Life), by Solomon b. Judah Ibn Gabirol (Avicebron), was translated in the twelfth century by a Dominican Monk Gudisalvi, with the help of a converted Jew, John Avendeath, into Latin, and since that time it has played an important rôle in the struggle between the Thomists and Scotists. Even Giordano Bruno consulted the Fons Vitae (Source of Life), the book of the Jewish philosopher Avicebron. More influential than the neo-Platonist, Avicebron, was Maimonides, whose book the *More Nebuchim* (Guide of the Perplexed), as shown by Dr. Joel, Professor of the Breslau Seminary, was greatly utilized by Albertus Magnus and Thomas Aquinas. According to Joel, the influence of Maimondian philosophy extended even to Leibnitz who, as recently shown by Foucher de Careil, was a devoted student and admirer of the More Nebuchim. "Even in Kant's Religious Philosophy," says Dr. Joel, "we sometimes detect an echo of the philosophy of Maimonides." (Cf. Frankel's *Monatsschrift fuer Geschichte und Wissenschaft de Judentums.* Jahrgang, 1860, pp. 205-217. Also Graetz: *Geschichte de Juden*, Vol. VI, pp.31-49 and p. 377.

national Humanitarianism is just as unfruitful as the anti-humanitarian Nationalism of Mediæval reaction. In theoretical anti-national humanitarianism I can only see, mildly speaking, an idealistic dream, but not a semblance of reality. We become so saturated with spiritualistic love and humanistic chloroform that we ultimately become entirely unconscious of the pain and misery that the antagonism which still exists between the various members of the great human family causes in real life. This antagonism will not be eradicated by enlightened sermons, but only by a process of historical development based on laws as unchangeable as the laws of Nature. Just as Nature does not produce flowers and fruits of a general character, nor general plants and animals, but produces particular plant and animal types, so does the creative power in history produce only folk types. In mankind, the plan of the plant and animal kingdoms finds its perfection; but humanity, as a separate life sphere, as the sphere of social life, is still in the process of development. We find in the history of social life a primal differentiation of folk-types which at first; plantlike, existed side by side with each other; then, animal-like, fought each other and destroyed or absorbed one another, but which will finally, in order to become absolutely free, live not only in friendly fashion with one another, but live *each for the other,* preserving, at the same time, their particular type identity.

The laws of universal history, I mean the history of the universe, namely, those of the cosmic, organic and social life, are as yet little known. We have particular sciences, but not a science of the universe; we still do not know the unity of all life. One thing, however, is certain, that a fusion of cults, an ideal to which so many aspire, and which was realized, at least in part, for thousands of years by Catholic Rome, will as little establish a lasting peace in human society as the philanthropic but unscientific belief in the absolute equality of men. In their attempt to base the granting of equal rights to all men on the primitive uniformity of all races and types, the humanitarians confound the organization of social life on the basis of solidarity, which is the result of a long and painful process of historical development, with a ready-made, inorganic equality and uniformity, which becomes rarer and rarer the farther back we go in history. The reconciliation of races follows its own natural laws, which we can neither arbitrarily create nor change. As to the fusion of cults, it is really a past stage in the development of social life. It was the watchword of that religion which, owes its existence to the death of the nations of antiquity, i.e., Christianity. To-day the real problem is how free the various oppressed races and folk-types and allow them to develop in their own way. The dangerous possibility that the various nationalities will separate themselves entirely from each other or ignore each other is to be feared as little as the danger that they will fight among themselves and enslave one another.

The present-day national movement not only does not exclude humanitarianism, but strongly asserts it; for this movement is a wholesome reaction, not against humanism, but against the things that would encroach upon it and cause its degeneration, against the leveling tendencies of modern industry and civilization which threaten to deaden every original organic life-force, by introducing a uniform inorganic mechanism. As long as these tendencies were directed against the antiquated institutions of a long-passed historical period, their existence was justified. Nor can this nationalistic reaction object to them, insofar as they endeavor to establish closer relations between the various nations of the world. But, fortunately, people have gone so far in life, as well as in science, as to deny the typical and the creative; and as a result the vapor of idealism, on the one hand, and the dust of atomism on the other, rest like mildew on the red corn, and stifle the germinating life in the bud. It is against these encroachments on the most sacred principles of creative life that the national tendencies of our time react, and it is against these destructive forces that I appeal to the original national power of Judaism.

Like the general universal cosmic life which finds its termination in it, and the individual microcosmic life in which all the buds and fruits of the spirit finally ripen. Humanity is a living organism, of which races and peoples are the members. In every organism changes are continually going on. Some, quite prominent in the embryonic stage, disappear in the later development. There are organs, on the other hand, hardly noticeable in the earlier existence of the organism, which become important only when the organism reaches the end of its development.

To the latter class of members of organic humanity (which class is really the creative one) belongs the Jewish people. This people was hardly noticeable in the world, where it was greatly oppressed by its powerful, conquering neighbors. Twice it came near being destroyed; namely, in the Egyptian and Babylonian captivities; and twice it rose to new spiritual life and fought long and successfully against the mightiest as well as the most civilized peoples of antiquity—the Greeks and the Romans. Finally, in the last struggle of the ancient world, it was this people which fertilized the genius of humanity with its own spirit, so as to rejuvenate itself, along with the regeneration of humanity. To-day, when the process of rejuvenation of the historical peoples is ended and each nation has its special function in the organism of humanity, we are for the first time beginning to conceive the England, with its industrial organization, represents the nerve-force of humanity which directs and regulates the alimentary system of mankind; France, that of general motion, namely, the social; Germany discharges the function of thinking; and America represents the general regenerating power by means of which all elements if the historical peoples will be assimilated into one. We observe that every modern people, every part of modern society, displays in its activity as an organ of humanity a special calling, then he must also determine the importance and function of the only ancient people which still exists to-day, as strong and vigorous as it was in days of old, namely, the people of Israel.

In the organism of humanity there are no two peoples which attract and repel each other more than the Germans and the Jews; just as there are no two mental attitudes which are simultaneously akin to each other and still diametrically opposed, as the scientific-philosophical and the religious-moral. Religion, in its higher form, is the spiritual tie which binds the creature to the Creator, the infinite thread, the end of which returns to its source, the bridge which leads from one creation to the other, from life to death, and from death back to life. It not only brings man to know the absolute more intimately, but it inspires and sanctifies his whole life with the divine spirit. In religion, as in love, especially in a religion like Judaism, which is neither one-sidedly materialistic nor one-sidedly spiritualistic, body and spirit merge into one I; another. The greatest and most dangerous enemy of the Jewish religion in antiquity was the religion of gross sensualist, the material love of the Semites, namely, Baal worship. In Mediæval ages, the enemy was represented by the embodiment of spiritualistic love—Christianity. The Jewish people which, thanks to its prophets of antiquity and rabbis of the Middle Ages, kept its religion from both extremes of degeneration, was, and is still today that organ of humanity which expresses the living, native force in universal history, namely, the organ of unifying and sanctifying love. This organ is akin to the organ of thought, but is, at the same time, opposed to it both draw their force from the inexhaustible well of life. But, while the religious genius individualizes the infinite, philosophic, scientific thought abstracts from life all its individual, subjective forms and generalizes it. Objective philosophy and science have no direct connection with life; religious teaching is intimately united with it, for either religion is identical with the national, social and moral life, or it is mere hypocrisy.

I have wandered from my trend of thought. I merely wanted to explain to you why I do not ally myself with the humanitarian aspirations which endeavor to obliterate all differentiation in the organism of humanity and in the name of such catch words as "Liberty" and "Progress," build altars to arbitrariness and ignorance, on which our light-minded youth offers its best energies and sacrifices.

Tenth Letter

Another dilemma—Experimental sciences—Philosophy and Religion—Progress and periodic circulation—A genetic comparison of the organic, cosmic life with the social—Moral necessity or holiness—Epochs of social evolution: the palæontological times of the formation of the embryo, birth period and birth travail, age of maturity.

Just as you confronted me on a former occasion with the dilemma: "Humanitarianism or Nationalism," and reproached me for sympathizing with national aspirations, in spite of the fact that they contradict the humanitarian tendencies of our time, so do you now propound another dilemma: "Freedom or Necessity." You think it pure fatalism to consider humanity as a higher organism, and to observe in the history of nations the operation of the same eternal laws which govern the history of the earth and Nature. You think that in cosmic and organic life, moral laws do not obtain; here only natural forces operate, which are predetermined, and which can be calculated beforehand. But it is different with social life. Even this life is regulated by natural conditions, but it is the goal of man, who is a free being, to overcome the fatalism of Nature with his free-will actions, which are the basis of morality and progress in the higher sense.

I am pleased to see that you are well versed in the higher philosophical conceptions of German thought. I agree with you in your view of human life and believe, also, that moral freedom is the destiny of man as well as of humanity. But to me this goal of humanity is identical with the recognition of God, which Judaism proclaimed at the very beginning of its history, and to the spread and development of which it has always contributed, and which, since Spinoza, it has made accessible to all historical nations. This knowledge of God, which in its first manifestations as the spirit of historical humanity, had not been fully conceived, but only perceived through unanalyzed sense impressions and intuitive experience, and which heretofore had appeared only as wisdom and light, must henceforth, on the basis of the already acquired wisdom and light, progress and become an exact science, which draws its knowledge not only from internal and external experience, but also examines it critically.

In order to forestall your criticism of my Jewish view of the world through arguments based upon speculative philosophy, I have no other choice but to prove to you that philosophic speculation is not the last word in mental development, as little as is industrial speculation and dominance of Capital the goal of material development. Exact science, which recognizes only observation, experience, work and research, as the only legitimate means of acquiring mental and material wealth, and considers speculation to be only a combination of mental trickery and unfounded hypothesis must, in my case, become the supreme authority to which I appeal. I will show you, that although exact science which recognizes only eternal natural laws, seems to be in apparent contradiction to philosophy, which raises spirit above nature, and to religion, which sanctifies *both spirit and nature,* insofar as it subordinates them both to a single being, yet it finally changes into that perfect knowledge, which conceives the laws of nature and history as one and the same, and where all contradiction disappears. But I must first make you understand that even this apparent contradiction between science and philosophy and religion had its justification, and was a necessary stage in the history of human development.[1]

---

[1]Cf. *Die genetische Weltanschauung.* Also *Resultat der Philosophie und der Erfahrungswissenschaften,* von M. Hess, in the periodical *Der Gedanke,* Vol. III, p. 103. See also Epilogue 4.

Even to-day, science, philosophy and religion are not reconciled to one another. On the contrary, to-day, when we are on the eve of a new historical era, just as in the corresponding critical transition period from antiquity to the Middle Ages, the seemingly irreconcilable antagonism between religion, philosophy and experimental science, is more marked than it was in the heyday of the ancient or Mediæval world, which hardly knew such an antagonism. The basis of this theoretical contradiction, just as the practical antagonism in social life, lies in the unequal development of the various classes of humanity, in the relations between the dominant and subservient races and classes, in the division of material and intellectual labor, and in the acquisitions resulting from this division. This inequality of development, advancing with the progress of civilization, was the rock upon which ancient society foundered. In the material and mental spheres, and especially in the latter, these contrasts, which ruined the ancient world, are more sharply defined to-day than they were at the close of the age of antiquity, when the division of labor was not as minutely developed as it is in our present transition period. The result is that today, as in the ancient world, not only is religion in conflict with philosophy, but philosophy is also antagonistic to exact science. And yet, as you will yourself admit, truth in experimental science cannot be different from truth in philosophy or in religion. But as long as the reconciliation between these various spheres of knowledge is not accomplished, it will be a difficult matter for me to prove to you, in a few lines, or even to make it plausible to you, that science, philosophy and religion do not mutually exclude each other; that at the worst, they only ignore each other; and that finally, they will support each other and with united forces help the progress of mankind.

Let us, then, first make clear to ourselves the oft-misunderstood concepts of "Freedom" and "Progress," which are so often carelessly used.

The belief in a rational, and therefore cognizable, divine Law, as revealed to humanity in the teaching and life of Judaism, this belief in a divine Providence, in a place of creation, is not a blind, fatalistic belief in destiny, although it excludes arbitrary and lawless freedom. I do not assert, with the materialists, that the organic and spiritual world is subjected, like the inorganic world, to the same laws as an external mechanism. On the contrary, I affirm that cosmic mechanical phenomena have the same plan, the same purposefulness, and spring out of the same sacred life as organic and spiritual phenomena. Nature and humanity are subordinated to the same divine law. The difference is, that Nature follows this law blindly, while man, when perfectly developed, obeys it consciously and voluntarily. Another important difference, the non-observance of which gives rise to a misunderstanding of the concepts of "freedom"; and "Progress," lies in this, that while the natural sphere of life of the organic and cosmic world, which is the basis of our social, human sphere of life, has already accomplished its own development, humanity is still in the midst of its life-creating process. As long as human society is still occupied in the production of its own organism, man, in his creative capacity, considers himself as an irresponsible and unfettered being, although he, like Nature, is subordinated, in his very creation, to the eternal divine laws. The false conception of human freedom as arbitrariness arises mainly from the fact that we do not as yet know either the laws regulating the development of social life or its goal; and we cannot know this law from experience so long as we are still in the midst of the stream of development.

But though science is still silent concerning the law governing the development of social life, the religious genius discovered it long ago. We Jews have always, from the beginning of our history, cherished the faith in a future Messianic epoch. This belief is symbolically expressed, in our historical religion, by the Sabbath festival. The celebration of the Sabbath is the embodiment of the great idea which has always animated us, namely, that the future will bring about the realization of the historical Sabbath, just as the past gave us the natural Sabbath. In other words, that History, like Nature, will finally have her epoch of harmonious perfection. The Biblical story of the Creation is told only for the sake of the Sabbath ideal. It tells us, in symbolic language, that when the creation of the world of Nature was completed, with the calling into life of the highest organic being of the earth—Man—and the Creator celebrated his natural Sabbath, there at once began the work-days of History. Then, also, began the history of creation of the social world, which will celebrate *its* Sabbath after the completion of its world-historical labor, by introducing the Messianic epoch. Here, in this conception, you can see the high moral value of the Mosaic genesis history, in which supernaturalists have discovered a system of science. As you see, my esteemed friend, the very biblical Sabbath-law in itself inspires us with a feeling of certainty that the uniform, eternal, divine law governs alike both the world of Nature and the world of History. It is only to those people who cannot conceive the manifestation of the religious genius of the Jews that the historical development of humanity appears as lawless, indeterminate, infinite "Progress" when contrasted with the life of Nature which, though it has not reached the end of its development, is yet governed by strict laws which are calculable. You see, however, that this apparent difference between the laws of Nature and those of history, is only the result of a subjective conception which cannot rise to an understanding of the great universal, divine laws. We can as little think of the freedom of the created being of History as mere lawless arbitrariness, as we can speak of the historical progress as infinite.

We call every being free, in the natural sense, which can develop its own destiny, its inner calling, according to its natural inclinations, without any external restraint. That being is free, in the moral sense, which follows its calling with consciousness and will, whose will coincides with the divine law will. Every other form of will is only arbitrariness, which does not partake of the divine essence of willing, but owes its existence to passions and natural instincts. This ability to follow the desires and passions which lead astray from the path of reason and morality, man possesses only when his inner essence is not sufficiently developed. Man can certainly not be proud of this negative ability, which is no more than a disease, a disease indicating a lack of development. This ability does not raise him above the animal, but on the contrary puts him below it; for animal life, as well as plant life, is already developed and perfected.

"Man," says Goethe, "errs as long as he strives." But there is no striving without a purpose. The goal to which humanity, in the course of its historical development, strives is the recognition of the laws which govern all the three life-spheres, the social, organic and cosmic.

The law of the universe is the law of generation and development, or to use a better-known expression, "the law of progress." The complete and perfect operation of this law, in all. the three life-spheres, is not yet known. In order to recognize fully the workings of this law, we still miss a part of its field of operation—the last phase of development of the social life. The law of history, therefore, cannot as yet become scientifically known. The ways of Providence are still but dimly outlined for us. But, thanks to the religious genius of the Jews and its divine Revelation, which continually manifested itself in various forms: first in prophetic utterances, then in mysticism, and finally in philosophic speculation—the human spirit was constantly brought nearer to the recognition of this law. It is, however, still necessary that the law of history should be investigated and its operations defined by the experimental sciences.

What modern science knows about the law of generation and development operating in the three life-spheres, the cosmic, organic and social, I have already discussed elsewhere.[2] But I have come to the conclusion, through my scientific and historical studies, that there is only one law governing all movement and life phenomena of all the spheres of the universe, the organisms of the earth and the nations of history. There is as little infinite, indeterminate progress in the social human world, as there is in the plant and animal world, at the end of which stands the natural, undeveloped man. Here, as in the cosmic life-sphere, the field of operation of which is infinite space,[3] everything is generated, develops, accomplishes its aim in life, and then decays and dissolves in order to arise again to a new life entity in the eternal, infinite, unified and divine cycle of universal life. What we call "progress" is no more than the development of a being from the germ stage to the mature life stage. At this stage each being reaches its destination.

Just as beings vary, just as the difference between the single atom and the entire world-sphere, between the lowest organic infusorium and the highest earthly being—Man— is wide and great, so various and wide is the difference between their ages of life maturity and consequently between their goals and destinations. But nothing living remains unchanged in time and space, nothing is eternal, everything comes into existence, and ultimately disappears after it has carried out its mission in order to arise again to a new form of life.[4]

The great planetary bodies originated and developed in a space and time of such magnitude that we have no standard of comparison wherewith to measure it. Organic life, which began to develop on these bodies after they had already cooled off and their surface had become rigid, consumed the entire palæontological age in its development and perfection. Finally, man, who began his spiritual, humane and social development at the ripe age of the organic life sphere, will reach his destination only after humanity will have completed its historical development which, though it has not reached its end as yet, is still not unlimited and infinite.

Whatever arises in time requires, of course, a certain time for its development, but it must reach its completion and perfection in a finite and determinate time. We recognize only one eternal, timeless and spaceless, absolute being. We infer its existence through the one absolute law governing natural and historical life, the revelation of which only Judaism possessed. Out of the unified recognition of this law a unified life will necessarily follow; for knowledge and action, or theory and life, are inseparable. Dualism, struggle, and even victory of virtue exist only during the historical development of the recognition of God, but not after its perfection. During this development, we are only able to strive *after* morality; but after the recognition of God, or his law is perfected within us, we must *live* morally. This moral necessity is holiness. Judaism, which from the beginning of its history revealed the unity and sacredness of the divine law in Nature and history, has, therefore, from the beginning, put forth the demand that holiness should become an ideal of life, and its prophets have always heralded the coming of the epoch when men will arrive at the full knowledge of God.[5]

---

[2]See Note VII at end of book.

[3]Cf. *Essai d'une genèse comparée de la vie cosmique, organique et sociale*, in the *Revue philosophique et religieuse*, for the years 1855-1856.

[4]Hess concedes the infinity of space as well as the infinity of life in the universe, but views this latter infinity not as a constant and given only as a recurrent and cyclical. In this view he was preceded by Heraclitus and the Stoics, but the novelty of the view consists in his introducing the creative factor, and in this he is the precursor of the Bergsonian conception of Creative Evolution. Cf. Introduction.—*Translator.*

[5]Cf. Leviticus xix, 2; Jeremiah xxxi, 31, 33, 45. All prophetic descriptions which Christinity has applied to itself, really characterize the epoch of a perfected human life dominated by the knowledge of God or by a perfect attitude toward holiness.

We must not represent either the sacred essence of God, or even our own God-like essence, in terms of time and space. The perfect recognition is, in reality, the overcoming of spatiality and temporality, namely, the historical development of the divine law in the cosmic, organic and social life spheres. We display our imperfect development and immature knowledge when we represent eternity as time continuance. Such representations prove only that our relation to holiness is not as yet perfect. The revelations of the holy spirit point to no other future but to the mature age of the social world. This age will begin, according to our historical religion, with the Messianic era. This is the era in which the Jewish nation and all the other historical nations will arise again to a new life, the time of the "resurrection of the dead," of "the coming of the Lord," of the "New Jerusalem," and of all the other symbolic expressions, the meaning of which is no longer misunderstood.

The Messianic era is the present age, which began to germinate with the teachings of Spinoza, and finally came into historical existence with the great French Revolution.[6] With the French Revolution, there began the regeneration of those nations which had acquired their national historical religion only through the influence of Judaism.

The social life-sphere, like the cosmic and the organic, is divided in its development into three epochs, which in their intrinsic structure are analogous in all the three life spheres. The first manifestation of history, that of ancient Judaism and Paganism, is the palæontological epoch of social life. It corresponds, on the one hand, to the embryological epoch in the history of development of organic life on this earth, which terminated in the tertiary period with the birth of the present existing organisms; and, on the other hand, it is analogous, in the cosmic sphere, to the epoch of world formation, the age of comets and nebulae, an age which finally culminated in the birth and rise of the astral bodies.

The second manifestation of history that of Mediæval Judaism, Christianity and Islam, is the epoch of the birth of modern Society. It corresponds, in the organic sphere, to the period of the birth of the present existing organisms, and in the cosmic world to the time of the birth of the planetary bodies.

The third manifestation of history, namely, the present age of the social life-sphere, corresponds to the epoch of perfected "organisms in the organic sphere and that of the developed planetary system in the cosmic.

This age of maturity began, in the cosmic sphere, with the satellites or double stars and ended with the perfection of the solar systems; in the organic sphere, it began with the prehistoric period, and finally came to completion in the historic races of mankind. In the social sphere, it is not yet completed; it is at present developing its last race and class struggle, in order to bring about a reconciliation of all opposites and to establish an equilibrium between production and consumption, and finally to reach that perfected and harmonious course of life which characterizes every age of maturity.

You will find, esteemed friend, the world-view, here outlined, to be the underlying basis of all my works. I have never held any other since I became a writer. It is the soul of my aspirations. Its realization is my life work, and at the opportune moment I hope to develop it further. The narrow limits of a letter do not allow more detailed discussion of such a broad subject. Besides, I am at present too much interested in the

[6]This view of the world I have already expressed in my first work, which appeared in the year 1836. (Cf. *The Sacred History of Mankind*, by a young Spinozist, where I wrote the following: "As the appointed period of the Mediæval terminated, there again rose the ancient voice of the Court of history: 'My spirit shall not strive with Man,' Gen. Vi, 3.)... There followed after Spinoza no dest"ructive flood of water, as after Adam, or a flood of tribes and peoples as after Christ, but out of the womb of time there burst forth a flood of ideas, which destroyed and wiped out every obstacle in its path... With the French Revolution, the third and last stage of development of humanity began, the process of which is not yet completed."

fate of my own people to devote myself to the solution of a problem which, though intrinsically connected with the future of Judaism, must first await the solution of the Jewish national problem.

ELEVENTH LETTER

Regenerated Judaism and the sacrificial cult—Two thousand year yearning of the nation for a new center in Zion—Patriotic songs and prayers—An old legend—Signs of the times —The time of return approaches—The Eastern Question and the Jews—A Frenchman's enthusiastic appeal.

You ask me to come back to earth from the starry regions of philosophy to the soil of Palestine. You certainly love the antithesis. As an offset to the noble and exalted historical religion of my regenerated Judaism, you oppose the "bloody sacrificial cult" of the ancient Israelites, and claim that orthodox Jews will never agree to a rebuilding of the Temple without, at the same time, reinstituting this ancient cult. You assume, therefore, that my love for my people will not go so far as to consent to an introduction of the sacrificial cult.

I cannot grant you, however, either the supposed *conditio sine qua non*, on the part of orthodox Jews, or your hypothetical conception of the degree of my patriotism. In regard to my deep, reawakened, though belated love for my people, it seems to me that you forget that real, strong love, the love which dominates body and spirit alike, is always blind. Its blindness consists in this, that it is not the perfection and excellent qualities of the beloved which are the object of love's desire, but the beloved being as it is, with all its good and bad traits. Love desires not the object of affection because it hopes to improve its bad traits, but because it loves the undivided, individual entity. The scar on the face of my beloved does not detract from my love for her, but is itself dear to me; dearer, perhaps, than her beautiful eyes, for other women may have beautiful eyes, but the scar is characteristic only of my beloved's individuality. Were, really, the sacrificial cult an inseparable part of Jewish nationality, I would unhesitatingly accept it. But as long as I have not learned anything better, I am convinced to the contrary. Our exalted historical religion, a religion which has progressed from one enlightened condition to another, which breathes only love for humanity and the knowledge of God,[1] cannot have the sacrificial cult as an essential part of its being. But in spite of my personal conviction, let me not venture to anticipate history. There are certain questions which *a priori*, namely, in a practical way, seem to be insolvable, but which, in the course of historical development, solve themselves. To such questions belongs also the question of cult in general, and the development of a definite form of divine worship out of the moral, religious spirit of that nation which, at every period of its development, was the creator of its own religion in particular.

Dr. Sachs, from whose classical work I have already cited excerpts, when speaking of the rigidity of the religious norms in exile and contrasting with this rigidity their former historical development on the soil of Palestine, says: "The ground of a living, historical reality is too wide to be encompassed by a ready-made system of norms and rules; nay, even the fixed norms themselves cannot withstand the strong influence of the free-moving expression of life and remain unchanged. The rushing current of a living movement undermines the obstructing dikes and penetrates by its windings and meanderings into the hard rocks of the shore." It is only after the extinction of the

[1] Brunsen remarks in his Biblical work, that the world progressed from light creation to light generation. If the Rabbinic phrase: "He prophesied but did not know what he prophesied" is ever applicable, it is applicable here. Bunsen hardly thought of our two thousand years' yearning for a new creation of light for Zion, which is expressed in our daily prayer, the *Shema*, etc. To Him that maketh the great luminaries we pray, "Cause a new light to shine upon Zion and may we all be worthy soon to enjoy its brightness." This *Shema* prayer is the jewel of our prayer book. Like a costly stone framed in purest gold, is the Shema surrounded by hymns and prayers such as *Ahaba Rabba, V'ahabta, Ahvath 'Olam,* all of which breathe love and reverence for knowledge.

national life of the people, which molded the religious norms in live fashion, that these norms have assumed a form of rigidity. But this rigidity will disappear from the religious life, as soon as the extinct national life comes into existence again, when the current of a national historical development forces itself anew into the hard and rigid religious forms.

The holy spirit, the creative genius of the people, out of which Jewish life and teaching arose, deserted Israel when its children began to feel ashamed of their nationality. But this spirit will again animate our people when it awakens to a new life, and creates new things of which we have at present not even a conception. No one can foretell what form and shape the newborn life and spirit of the regenerated nations will assume. As regards the religious cult, and especially the Jewish cult, it will certainly be different from the present as well as from the ancient form.

Regarded by itself, the sacrificial cult, as described in the Bible, does not contain anything repellent to the spirit of humanitarianism. On the contrary, as compared with the horrible custom of human sacrifices practiced by all the nations of antiquity, the Jewish practice of animal sacrifices was a splendid victory for the spirit of humanitarianism.[2] Be that as it may, whether animal sacrifices are regarded as a concession on the part of the Torah to Paganism, in order to prevent a relapse on the part of the people into idolatry, or whether it be maintained that it contains a hidden symbolism, the meaning of which is at present unknown, one thing is well established, that the Jews, in spite of their having brought "bloody sacrifices," possess greater abhorrence for bloodshed and the eating of blood than modern nations which consume the blood together, with the meat, without sacrifice or ceremony. But the sacrificial cult has not been practiced for the last eighteen hundred years, and therefore our new-fashioned Jews are ashamed of it. And yet it seems that even to the present day, sacrifice is the natural expression of the pious spirit of the child. Goethe tells us, that in his childhood, the only way he could satisfy his religious craving was by means of sacrifice to the Eternal, which he performed by lighting a bonfire and throwing therein his favorite toys.

On the other hand, the prophets of old, and even the rabbis of the Middle Ages, never considered the sacrificial cult essential to the Jewish religion as do modern rigidly orthodox Jews, who look upon it as inseparable from our national restoration. Rabbi Jochanan ben Zakkai declared, basing his utterance on the prophetic saying in Hosea vi 6, that sacrifices can be substituted by benevolence,[3] and a number of modern rabbinical authorities, who do not recognize the right of the modern descendants of Aaron to the priesthood, have yet declared themselves zealously for the restoration of a Jewish State.[4] The cult that we are going to introduce in the New Jerusalem can and must, for the present, remain an open question. Rome was not built in a day, and the New Jerusalem must needs take time for its construction.

What we have to do at present for the regeneration of the Jewish nation is, first, to keep alive the hope of the political rebirth of our people, and next, to reawaken that hope where it slumbers. When political conditions in the Orient shape themselves so as to permit the organization of a beginning of the restoration of a Jewish State, this beginning will express itself in the founding of Jewish colonies in the land of their ancestors, to which enterprise France will undoubtedly lend a hand. You know how substantial was the share of the Jews in the subscriptions to the fund raised for the benefit of the Syrian war victims. It was Cremieux who took the initiative in the

---

[2]See Note VIII at end of book.

[3]For the saying of Ben Zakkai, see Baba Bathra, 10b.—*Translator.*

[4]See Note X at end of book.

matter, the same Cremieux who twenty years ago traveled with Sir Moses Montefiore to Syria in order to seek protection for the Jews against the persecutions of the Christians. In the *Journal des Debats*, which very seldom accepts poems for publication, there appeared, at the time of the Syrian expedition, a poem by Leon Halevi, who at the time, perhaps, thought as little of the rebirth of Israel as Cremieux, yet his beautiful stanzas could not have been produced otherwise than in a spirit of foreseeing this regeneration. When the poet of the *Schwalben* mournfully complains:

Where tarries the hero? Where tarries the wise?
Who will, O my people, revive you anew;
Who will save you, and give you again
A place in the sun?

The French poet answers his query with enthusiastic confidence:

Ye shall be reborn, ye fearsome cities!
A breath of security will always hover
O'er your banks where our colors have fluttered!
Come again a call supreme!
Au revoir is not adieu—
France is all to those she loves,
The future belongs to God.

Alexander Weill sang about the same time:

There is a people stiff of neck,
Dispersed from the Euphrates to the Rhine,
Its whole life centered in a Book—
Oft times bent, yet ever straightened;
Braving hatred and contempt,
It only dies to live again
In nobler form.

France, beloved friend, is the savior who will restore our people to its place in universal history.

Allow me to recall to your mind an old legend which you have probably heard in your younger days. It runs as follows:

"A knight who went to the Holy Land to assist in the liberation of Jerusalem, left behind him a very dear friend. While the knight fought valiantly on the field of battle, his friend spent his time, as heretofore, in the study of the Talmud, for his friend was none other than a pious rabbi."

"Months afterward, when the knight returned home, he appeared suddenly at midnight, in the study room of the rabbi, whom he found, as usual, absorbed in his Talmud. 'God's greetings to you, dear old friend,' he said. 'I have returned from the Holy Land and bring you from there a pledge of our friendship. What I gained by my sword, you are striving to obtain with your spirit our ways lead to the same goal.' While thus speaking, the knight handed the rabbi a rose of Jericho."

"The rabbi took the rose and moistened it with his tears, and immediately the withered rose began to bloom again in its full glory and splendor. And the rabbi said to the knight: 'Do not wonder, my friend that the withered rose bloomed again in my hands. The rose possesses the same characteristics as our people: it comes to life again at the touch of the warm breath of love, in spite of its having been torn from its own soil and left to wither in foreign lands. So will Israel bloom again in youthful splendor; and the spark, at present smoldering under the ashes, will burst once more into a bright flame.'"

The routes of the rabbi and the knight dear friend, are meeting to-day. As the rabbi in the story symbolizes our people, so does the knight of the legend signify the French people which in our days, as in the Middle Ages, sent its brave soldiers to Syria and "prepared in the desert the way of the Lord."

Have you never read the words of the Prophet Isaiah: "Comfort ye, comfort ye, my people, saith your God. Speak ye comfortably to the heart of Jerusalem, and cry unto her, that the appointed time has come, that her iniquity is pardoned; for she hath received at the Lord's hand double for all her sins. The voice of one that crieth in the wilderness; prepare ye the way of the Lord, make straight in the desert a highway for our God. Every valley shall be exalted, and every mountain and hill shall be mad low, and the crooked shall be made a straight place, and the rough places a plain. And the glory of the Lord shall be revealed, and all flesh shall see it together: for the mouth of the Lord hath spoken it."[5]

Do you not believe that in these words, with which second Isaiah opened his prophecies, as well as in words with which the Prophet Obadiah closed his prophecy,[6] the conditions of our own time are graphically pictured? Was not help given to Zion in order to defend and establish the wild mountaineers there? Are not things being prepared there and roads leveled, and is not the road of civilization being built in the desert in the form of the Suez Canal works and the railroad which will connect Asia and Europe? They are not thinking at present of the restoration of our people. But you know the proverb, "Man proposes and God disposes." Just as in the West they once searched for a road to India, and incidentally discovered a new world, so will our lost fatherland be rediscovered on the road to India and China that is now being built in the Orient. Do you still doubt that France will help the Jews to found colonies which may extend from Suez to Jerusalem, and from the banks of the Jordan to the Coast of the Mediterranean? Then pray read the work which appeared shortly after the massacres in Syria, by the famous publisher, Dentu, under the title *The New Oriental Problem*. The author hardly wrote it at the request of the French government, but acted in accordance with the spirit of the French nation when he urged our brethren, not on religious grounds, but from purely political and humanitarian motives, to restore their- ancient State.[7]

I may, therefore, recommend this work, written, not by a Jew, but by a French patriot, to the attention of our modern Jews, who plume themselves on borrowed French humanitarianism. I will quote here, in translation, a few pages of this work, *The New Eastern Question,* by Ernest Laharanne.[8]

"In the discussion of these new Eastern complications, we reserved a special place for Palestine, in order to bring to the attention of the world the important question, whether ancient Judæa can once more acquire its former place under the sun."

"This question is not raised here for the first time. The redemption of Palestine, either by the efforts of international Jewish banker, or the nobler method, of a general subscription in which all the Jews should participate, has been discussed many times. Why is it that this patriotic project has not as yet been realized? It is certainly not the fault of pious Jews that the plan was frustrated, for their hearts beat fast and their eyes

---

[5]Isaiah xl, 1-5.

[6]"And saviors shall come up on Mount Zion to judge the mount of Esau; and the kingdom shall be the Lord's."

[7]I have heard that an American writer has discussed this question from a practical point of view, for a number of years. Also representative Englishmen have repeatedly declared themselves in favor of the restoration of the Jewish State.

[8]See Note IX at end of book.

fill with tears at the thought of a return to Jerusalem."[9]

"If the project is still unrealized, the cause is easily cognizable. The Jews dare not think of the possibility of possessing again the land of their fathers. Have we not opposed to their wish our Christian veto? Would we not continually molest the legal proprietor when he will have taken possession of his ancestral land, and in the name of piety make him feel that his ancestors forfeited the title to their land on the day of the Crucifixion?"

"Our stupid Ultra-montanism has destroyed the possibility of a regeneration of Judæa, by making the present of the Jewish people barren and unproductive. Had the city of Jerusalem been rebuilt by means of Jewish capital, we would have heard preachers prophesying, even in our progressive nineteenth century, that the end of the world is at hand and predictions of the coming of the Anti-Christ. Yes, we have lived to see such a state of affairs, now that Ultra-montanism has made its last stand in oratorical eloquence. In the sacred beehive of religion, we still hear a continuous buzzing of those insects who would rather see a mighty sword in the hands of the barbarians, than greet the resurrection of nations and hail the revival of a free and great thought inscribed on their banner. This is undoubtedly the reason why Israel did not make any attempt to become master of his own flocks, why the Jews, after wandering for two thousand years, are not in a position to shake the dust from their weary feet. The continuous, inexorable demands that would be made upon a Jewish settlement, the vexatious insults that would be heaped upon them and which would finally degenerate into persecutions, in which fanatic Christians and pious Mohammedans would unite in brotherly accord—these are the reasons, more potent than the rule of the Turks, that have deterred the Jews from attempting to rebuild the Temple of Solomon, their ancient home, and their State."

"But if this cause explains the lack of courage on the part of patriotic Jews, we cannot refrain from accusing the so-called progressive Jews of indifference to the fate of the Jewish people; for whenever a project for the restoration of the Jewish State is being considered, they display toward it a naïveté that neither does credit to their reasoning power nor to their heart. The explanations offered by them on such occasions are inadmissible both from a moral and from a political point of view. A declaration, composed by the representatives of the progressive Jews at their meeting in Frankfort, contains the following Article:

'We acknowledge as our fatherland only the land where we are born and to which we are inseparably united by the bonds of citizenship.'"[10]

"No member of the Jewish race can renounce the incontestable and fundamental right of his people, without at the same time denying the history of the Jews and his own ancestors. Such an act is especially unseemly, at a time when political conditions in

[9]My friend, Armond L., who traveled for several years through the Danube Principalities, told me that the Jews were moved to tears when he announced to them the end of their suffering, with the words "The time of the return approaches." The more fortunate Occidental Jews do not know with what longing the Jewish masses of the East await the final redemption from the two thousand year exile. They know not that the patriotic Jew cannot suppress his cry of anguish at the length of the exile, even in the midst of his festive songs, as, for instance, the patriotic poem which is read on Chanukah, closes with the mournful call:

"For salvation is delayed for us and there is no end to the days of evil."

"They asked me,"continued my friend, "what are the indications that the end of the exile is approaching?" "These," I answered, "that the Turkish and papal powers are on the point of collapse."

[10]I do not know to which declaration the author refers. It is perhaps to one of the Rabbinical conference which took place in the year 1845 at Frankfort and which accomplished as much as a similar German meeting held in the same place a few years later. However, the declaration referred to is in perfect accord with the sentiments of the German progressive Jews. There was not a voice raised among them in behalf of the restoration of the Jewish nationality; and if such a voice is heard from other quarters, it is received by them not only with indifference, but with scorn.

Europe will not only not obstruct the restoration of a Jewish State, but will rather facilitate its realization. What European power to-day would oppose the plan that the Jews, united through a Congress, should buy back their ancient fatherland? Who would object if the Jews flung to decrepit old Turkey a few handfuls of gold, and said to her: 'Give me back my home and use this money to consolidate the other parts of your tottering empire?'

"No objections would be raised to the realization of such a plan, and Judæa would be permitted to extend its boundaries from Suez to the harbor of Smyrna, including the entire area of the western Lebanon range. For We will not be eternally engaged in war; the time must come when this wholesale massacre, usually accompanied by the booming of cannon, will be condemned by humanity, so that the nation which desires conquest in addition to commerce, will not dare to carry out its designs. We must therefore prepare and break new ground for the peaceful struggles of industry. European industry has daily to search for new markets as an outlet for its products. We have no time to lose. The time has arrived when it is imperative to call the ancient nations back to life, so as to open new highways and byways for European civilization."

In another passage, the author speaks with so much enthusiasm, love and reverence for the Jews, that what he says overshadows all that has ever been said by a Jew in praise of his own people.

"There is a mysterious power which rules the destiny of humanity. Once the hand of the Infinite Power has signed the decree of a nation to be banished forever from the fact of the earth, the fate of that nation is irrevocable. But when we see a nation, torn from its cradle in its early childhood, and after having tasted all the bitterness of exile is brought back to its land, only to be tossed again into the wide world; and that nation, during the eighteen centuries of its wandering has displayed such remarkable powers of endurance, suffering age-long martyrdom without extinguishing in its heart the fire of patriotism, then we just admit that we are standing before an infinite mystery, unparalleled in the history of humanity."

In these few words there is concentrated the whole history of Israel.

What an example! What a race! You, Roman conquerors, led your legions in battle against the already ruined Zion and drove the children of Israel out of their ancestral land. Your European, Asiatic and African barbarians lent your ear to superstition and pronounced your curse upon them. You, feudal kings, branded the Jews with the mark of shame—the Jews, who, in spite of all your persecutions, supplied you with the necessary gold wherewith to arm your vassals and serfs and who provided your markets with goods. You, grand Inquisitors, searched among the children of the dispersed people of Israel for your richest victims, with whom to fill your prisons and coffers, and in order to feed your auto-da-fe's—and you revoked the edict of Nantes[11] and drove out of the land the remnant that had escaped the destruction of Apostolic fanaticism. And finally, you modern nations have denied these indefatigable workers and industrious merchants civil rights. What persecutions! What tears! What blood you children of Israel have shed in the last eighteen hundred years! But you sons of Judæa, in spite of all suffering are still here. You have overcome the innumerable obstacles which the hatred, contempt, fanaticism and barbarism of the centuries have placed in your way. The hand of the Eternal has surely guided you.

France finally freed you. On the eve of the great world epoch, France, while shattering its own chains, called all nations and also you, into freedom. You became citizens and

[11]The edict of Nantes guaranteed the Prostestants of France liberty of conscience, freedom of worship and representation in Parliament; it was issued by Henry IV in 1593, but revoked by Louis XIV in 1685.— *Translator.*

now you are brothers. The year 1789 was the first step in the process of rehabilitation. Pursuing its mission, liberation,[12] the eye of France searched after all persecuted races, and it found you in your ghetto and shattered its doors forever.[13] France invited you to its Chambers. You participated in its triumphs; you shared its happiness and its reverses. You have raised your voice on the day of council, shouted for joy at our victories and wept at our defeats. You are good citizens and devoted brothers. France will perhaps be to you a lighthouse of salvation, a rock against your enemies, who are also the enemies of our modern institutions. It will defend you against the libelers of your nationality, your character and your religion.

You are an elemental force and we bow our heads before you. You were powerful in the early period of your history, strong even after the destruction of Jerusalem, and mighty during the Middle Ages, when there were only two dominant powers—the Inquisition and its Cross, and Piracy with its Crescent. You have escaped destruction in your long dispersion, in spite of the terrible tax you have paid during eighteen centuries of persecution. But what is left of your nation is mighty enough to rebuild the gates of Jerusalem. This is your mission. Providence would not have prolonged your existence until to-day, had it not reserved for you the holiest of all missions. The hour has struck for the resettlement of the banks of the Jordan. The historical books of the royal prophets can, perhaps, be written again only by you.

A great calling is reserved for you: to be a living channel of communication between three continents. You should be the bearers of civilization to the primitive people of Asia, and the teachers of the European sciences to which your race has contributed so much. You should be the mediators between Europe and far Asia, open the roads that lead to India and China—those unknown regions which must ultimately be thrown open to civilization. You will come to the land of your fathers crowned with the crown of age-long martyrdom, and there, finally, you will be completely healed from all your ills! Your capital will again bring the wide stretches of barren land under cultivation; your labor and industry will once more turn the ancient soil into fruitful valleys, reclaim the flat lands from the encroaching sands of the desert, and the world will again pay its homage to the oldest of peoples.

The time has arrived for you to reclaim, either by way of compensation or by other means, your ancient fatherland from Turkey, which has devastated it for ages. You have contributed enough to the cause of civilization and have helped Europe on the path of progress, to make revolutions and carry them out successfully. You must henceforth think of yourselves, of the valleys of Lebanon and the plains of Gennesareth.

March forward! At the sight of your rejuvenation, our hearts will beat fast, and our armies will stand by you, ready to help.

March forward, Jews of all lands! The ancient fatherland of yours is calling you, and we will be proud to open its gates for you.

March forward, ye sons of the martyrs! The harvest of experience which you have

---

[12]Under the short Napoleonic reign over Central and Southern Europe, despotism and autocracy were crushed everywhere; either republics or constitutional monarchies were substituted, and the Jews were granted equal rights, which were later revoked when the old dynasties were restored to the throne.—*Translator.*

[13]The old Beneday, who was still alive in 1843, at the time of the publication of the first *Rhenische Zeitung* used to come, from time to time, to the office of that paper to converse with the members of the staff; and on one of these occasions he told us the story, which I had really heard before, how he, at the commission of the first French Republic had laid the ax at the gates of the Bonn Ghetto. Beneday could hardly conceive how his son Jacob could, at one and the same time, be a liberal and yet unfriendly toward the French. I comforted him by pointing to the progressive German Jews, who in reality have to thank the French for whatever political and civil rights they possess here or elsewhere in Germany, and yet rail, in company with the Germans, against the "hereditary enemy."

accumulated in your long exile, will help to bring again to Israel the splendor of the Davidic days and rewrite that part of history of which the monoliths of Semiramis are the only witness.

March forward, ye noble hearts! The day on which the Jewish tribes return to their fatherland will be epoch making in the history of humanity. Oh, how will the East tremble at your coming! How quickly, under the influence of labor and industry, will the enervation of the people vanish, in the land where voluptuousness, idleness and robbery have held sway for thousands of years.

You will become the moral stay of the East. You have written the Book of books. Become, then, the educators of the wild Arabian hordes and the African peoples. Let the ancient wisdom of the East, the revelations of the Zend, the Vedas, as well as the more modern Koran and the Gospels, group themselves around your Bible. They will all become purified from every superstition and all will proclaim alike the principles of freedom, humanity, peace and unity. You are the triumphal arch of the future historical epoch, under which the great covenant of humanity will be written and sealed in your presence as the witnesses of the past and future. The Biblical traditions which you will revive, will also sanctify anew our Occidental society and destroy the weed of materialism together with its roots.

And when you shall have made this wonderful progress, remember, ye sons of Israel, remember Modern France which, from the moment of its rebirth, has loved you continually and has never wearied of defending you.

Twelfth Letter

The beginning of the end—Solidarity of the Jews—Philanthropic illusions—The social animal kingdom—The nurses of progress—The faithful watchmen of the sacred sepulchre of Jewish nationality—The last catastrophe.

It seems that extracts from the French pamphlet which I quoted to you, have awakened in you new thoughts. You think that the Christian nations will certainly not object to the restoration of the Jewish State, for they will thereby rid their respective countries of a foreign population which is a thorn in their side. Not only Frenchmen, but Germans and Englishmen, have expressed themselves more than once in favor of the return of the Jews to Palestine. You quote an Englishman who endeavored to prove, by Biblical evidence, the ultimate return of the Jews to Palestine and simultaneously also the conversion of the Jews to Christianity. Another Englishman attempts to prove that the present English dynasty is directly descended from the house of David and that the stone which plays such an important rôle in the coronation of English kings is the same on which Jacob's head rested when he dreamt of the famous ladder. A third magnanimously offers all the English ships for the purpose of conveying to Palestine, free of charge, all the Jews who want to return there. These sentiments, however, seem to be, according to you, only a milder form of the desire, which in former ages expressed itself in frequent banishments of the Jews from Christian lands, for which mildness our people ought to be thankful. On the other hand, you see in such projects only a piece of folly which, in its final analysis, leads either to religious or secular insanity, and should not be taken into consideration. Such desires, moreover, if they come from pious Christians, would be opposed by all Jews. On the other hand, if pious Jews were the projectors, all Christians would object to the restoration; for as the latter would only consent to a return to Palestine on condition that the ancient sacrificial cult be reintroduced in the New Jerusalem, so would the former give its assistance to the plan, only on condition that we Jews would bring our national religion as a sacrifice to Christianity at the "Holy Sepulchre." And thus, you conclude, all the national aspirations of the Jews must inevitably founder on the rock of differences of opinion.

Now if rigid Christian dogma and inflexible Jewish orthodoxy could never be revived by the living current of history, they would certainly place an insurmountable obstacle to the realization of our patriotic aspirations. The thought of repossessing our ancient fatherland can, therefore, be taken under serious consideration, only when this rigidity of orthodox Jews and Christians alike, will have relaxed. And it is beginning to relax already, not only with the progressive elements, but even with pious Jews and Christians. Moreover, the Talmud, which is the corner-stone of modern Jewish orthodoxy, long ago counseled obedience to the dictates of life.

If Jewish Nationalism is a live movement, it will not be deterred by any doubts that may arise from devoting its energy toward obtaining political regeneration. Though the time "when the wolf shall dwell with the lamb" has not yet arrived, the ruling majority and the oppressed minority have both alike lost their wolfish appetite and sheepish patience. Religious toleration has become a more general article of creed than any other dogma. Besides, I always think, as I have already remarked, of the future cult of all regenerated nations as being different in form from the present religious cults, which have come down to us from a time when folk individualities were repressed. And finally I must emphasize it again, our future religious worship, like those of other nations, will not precede the regeneration but follow it. The main problem of the Jewish national movement is not of a religious nature but centers around one point, namely, on how to awaken the patriotic sentiments in the hearts of our progressive Jews, and how to liberate the Jewish masses, by means of this patriotism, from a spirit-deadening formalism. If we succeed in this beginning, then no matter how difficult the practical realization of our plan may be, the difficulties will be overcome by experience itself. It is only when we find that the Jewish heart is dead, that the Jews are no more capable of patriotic inspiration, that we shall have to despair of our hope which, as every great historical ideal, cannot be realized without a tremendous struggle.

The Jews have enough common sense, in spite of misunderstood enlightenment and orthodoxy, not to be misled by religious haziness and fanaticism which have no basis in the present life. But it is just this sober sense of reality that our race possesses in a high degree, which will finally win over those of our brethren, whether progressive or orthodox, who still possess a Jewish heart, to the national cause which has its roots deep in the practical soil of reality.

The objections of progressive Jews to the restoration of the Jewish State have their ultimate ground, not in that spiritual education which does not shrink from the difficulties lying in the path of a great work, nor calculates beforehand the amount of sacrifice required in the realization of the same, but they rest in the moral and intellectual narrow-mindedness which is unable to rise to a high humanitarian standpoint, from which one can view the depth of the misfortune of the people as well as the means of their salvation. The Jewish religion, thought Heine, and with him all the enlightened Jews, is more of a misfortune than a religion. But in vain do the progressive Jews persuade themselves that they can escape this misfortune through enlightenment or conversion. Every Jew is, whether he wishes it or not, solidly united with the entire nation; and only when the Jewish people will be freed from the burden which it has borne so heroically for thousands of years, will the burden of Judaism be removed from the shoulders of these progressive Jews, who will ultimately form only a small minority. We will all then carry the yoke of the "Kingdom of Heaven" until the end.

At the height of the movement of enlightenment, when everybody was intoxicated by it, people could be easily fascinated by the illusion that it is best for the entire Jewish people to surrender its national religion and devote itself to humanitarianism, a cult which, according to them, was destined to absorb Judaism as well as all individual life; To-day, even the most superficial rationalist cannot cherish such a philanthropic illusion. Though lacking a deeper conception of life, of Nature and history, the historical movement among our contemporary Jews has accomplished its purpose of opening the eyes of the rationalists; for even in the Occident, where the Jews are closely united to the general culture by a thousand bonds, the injury done to the ancient Jewish cult by enlightenment is slight.

Even to-day, the great majority of Occidental Jews pay homage to their ancient religion. Neither emancipation nor Christian proselytism, with its bait of material advantages, has succeeded in estranging the majority of Jews from their traditions. On the contrary, there have appeared of late, even among those who were formerly estranged from Judaism, men who display strong sympathies for the ancient Jewish mode of life. The leveling tendencies of the assimilationists have remained and will always remain without influence on those Jews who constitute the great Jewish masses.

The masses are never moved to progress by mere abstract conceptions; the springs of action lie far deeper than even the socialist revolutionaries think. With the Jews, more than with other nations which, though oppressed, yet live on their own soil, all political and social progress must necessarily be preceded by national independence. A common, native soil is a primary condition, if there is to be introduced among the

74

Jews better and more progressive relations between Capital and Labor. The social man, just as the social plant and animal, needs for his growth and development a wide, free soil; without it, he sinks to the status of a parasite, which feeds at the expense of others. The parasitic way of existence has played an important rôle in the development of human history and is by no means restricted to the Jews. As long as science and industry were not sufficiently developed, the land in the possession of any nation was never large enough to maintain the entire population; and the nations were therefore forced, either to make war one upon the other and thus acquire slaves, or to divide their own population into ruling and serving classes. But this regime, which was based upon the exploitation of men, collapsed as soon as modern science and industry began to dominate the world.

The civilized nations are at present making preparations for a common exploitation of Nature. This will be carried on by means of labor based on scientific principles, all social parasites being excluded. They are preparing themselves for the new era through struggles for free national soils, by attempts at abolishing race and class rule, by endeavoring to organize an Association and by the cooperation of all the forces of production. In this Association, the antagonism between capitalistic speculation and productive labor, as well as the contrast between philosophic speculation and scientific work, will simultaneously disappear. I know well that the need of wholesome and just labor conditions, which should be based solely on the exploitation of Nature by man, is also strongly felt in Jewry. I know of the great efforts which are being exerted on the part of the Jews to train our younger generation as useful laborers. But I know also that the Jews in exile, at least the majority of them, cannot devote themselves successfully to productive labor; in the first place, because they lack the most necessary condition—an ancestral soil; and, secondly, because they cannot assimilate with the peoples among whom they live without at the same time denying their national religion and tradition. Those commendable efforts to improve the condition of Jewish labor will, therefore, while they indirectly cause the destruction of the Jewish cult, be as fruitless, on the whole, as the endeavors of the Reform movement, which leads directly to the same result. In exile, the Jewish people cannot be regenerated. Reform or philanthropy can only bring it to apostasy and to nothing else, but in this no reformer, not even a tyrant will ever succeed. The Jewish people will participate in the great historical movement of present-day humanity only when it will have its own fatherland. As long as the great Jewish masses remain in their low position, even the relatively few Jews who have surrendered their national traditions, in order to escape the fate of the Jewish people, will be more painfully affected by the position of the Jews than the masses, who feel themselves only unfortunate but not degraded. Hence, no Jew, whether orthodox or not, can conscientiously refrain from cooperating with the rest for the elevation of the entire Jewry. Every Jew, even the converted, should cling to the cause and labor for the regeneration of Israel.

If one appreciates fully the infinitely tragic rôle which the Jewish people has thus far played in history, he must also inevitably perceive the only way that will bring salvation to our misery. This solution is at present not as impractical as it may look at first sight. It is in accordance with the sympathies of the French people and with the interests of French politics, that after France's victorious armies shall have overthrown the modern Nebuchadnezzar, France will extend its, work of redemption also to the Jewish nation. It is to the interest of France to see that the road leading to India and China should be settled by a people which will be loyal to the cause of France to the end, in order that it may fulfill the historical mission which has fallen to it as a legacy from the great Revolution. But is there any other nation more adapted to carry out this mission than Israel, which was appointed for the same mission from the beginning of its history?

"Frenchmen and Jews!" I hear you exclaim. "If so, then the Christian German reactionaries were right in their denunciations of the Jews!" Yes, my dear friend, the animal instinct which scents the enemy in the distance is always infallible. Reaction has everywhere recognized its mortal enemy in those who stand midway between reaction and revolution and who act as the midwife of progress, the giant who is to smite reaction over its head. For it is a law of organic and social life history, that the mediate being whose existence is limited to the transition epoch, should pave the way from the imperfect to the more perfect and higher scales of life.

Frenchmen and Jews! It seems that in all things they were created for one another. They resemble one another in their humane and national aspirations, and differ only in such qualities as can only be complemented by another nation, but which are never united in one and the same people. The French people excel in alertness, in the humanistic and sympathetic quality to assimilate all elements; the Jews, on the other hand, possess more ethical seriousness than the French, and in meeting other types, the Jew will rather impress his stamp on his environment than be molded by it. The French can rule the world because they absorbed the best of the entire human race. The Jews can only be masters of their own flock, and with the holy fire which they have kindled in their own midst, they will warm and enlighten a world composed of heterogeneous elements, and thus prevent this world from disintegrating into its elements and relapsing into the chaos out of which it was raised once before by Judaism.

The generous help which France has extended to civilized peoples toward the restoration of their nationality, will be remembered longer by our nation than by any other. How easily will we come to an understanding with this humane French people about our religion and its sacred places in Palestine. But matters have not gone so far yet. The Jewish people must first show itself worthy of the regeneration of its historical cult; it must first feel the necessity of a national restoration if it would reach that point. Until then we need not think about building the Temple; we must win the heart of our brethren for the great work which will finally bring eternal glory to the Jewish nation and salvation to humanity.

For Jewish colonization on the road to India and China, there is no lack, either of Jewish laborers or of Jewish talent and capital. Let only the germ be planted under the protection of the European powers, and the tree of a new life will spring forth by itself and bear excellent fruit.

You smile at my innocent belief in Jewish patriotism. You have undoubtedly read the *Ghetto Scenes* and you will possibly remind me of the hero, Mendel Wilna, who possessed a fixed idea to persuade the Rothschilds to devote their capital and energy to the rebuilding of the Holy City and Temple, but who only succeeded in winning over a child to his pious belief. The child, when he grew up and attended the University became so wise that he concluded that only children and fools can dream of rebuilding Jerusalem. By quoting this episode, you wish to demonstrate that the Jewish poet did not see any deeper meaning in the patriotic feeling of pious Jews than considering them merely as a kind of Jewish Christmas trees, able to amuse only little children and elderly fools. All this, dearest friend, is true, but it applies only to the modern poet who is influenced by the Germanic spirit and not to a poet like Judah Halevi, who poured out his heart's blood in his Jewish poetry. Halevi, actuated by longing for the land of his dreams, grasped the pilgrim's staff, only to find a grave for himself in his beloved land. Nor does the poet's description characterize real Jewish life. You certainly remember the proverb: "Children and fools tell the truth." The thought which inspired the nervous Mendel Wilna and little Moischele, has been the fundamental thought of all pious Jews from the time of the destruction of Jerusalem until the present day. And there are such Jews—let it not worry Mr. Kompert, even among the Rothschild brothers.

But you do not need to overlook the fact that Kompert puts the denial of Jewish nationality into the mouth of a student who, when doubting the regeneration of the Jewish people, only reflects the sceptical spirit of the age. What progressive Jew, especially in Germany, would have dared within recent years to declare himself for the restoration of our nation and face his own friends, who would undoubtedly have declared him mad? In addition, I wish to remark that Kompert bestowed upon the Jewish student, who is theoretically indifferent, but practically devoted to the Jewish nation,—not without purpose—a Bohemian friend who is theoretically inspired by the example of Huss and Zizka, but who becomes ultimately a well-to-do monk, and exchanges the cup and sword for the cross and incense bowl. I do not find, therefore, in Kompert's description of the progressive Jews, any more of that extreme indifference with which, until recently, a great part of German Jewry was charged. Today, as I have said, we cannot accuse them of it without reserve. Remember, dear friend, that I was you who criticized my severe judgment of the progressive German Jews, a criticism to which I must do justice now. I have adapted the wholesome reaction of Jewish patriotism and asserted it in the face of an extreme indifference which had its seat more in "fashion" and in the spirit of the age, than in the heard of the people; and finally it struck root. The longing for the land of our forefathers and the desire to return there which is so strongly displayed by our pious brethren, who even in our days visit the Holy Land in order to be buried there, has finally affected even the heart of our progressive Jews. The frequent journeys to Jerusalem, the support given to our brethren there, the help extended to the educational and charitable institutions in Palestine, all these do not come only from orthodox Jews. These earnest and lasting endeavors to help our brethren in the Orient show that to-day there is no lack of good will among all classes of Jews, to alleviate the misery of their brethren in the Holy Land. This will need only to ripen in the formation of a plan to carry out the great patriotic work.

In Jerusalem, as everywhere, our Jewish philanthropists are confronted with insurmountable difficulties whenever they wish to solve the historical misfortune of our brethren by means of charitable institutions and distributions of alms, or when they expect to introduce moral-spiritual progress among the Oriental Jews by means of theoretical educational doctrines, without any social bases. The acquisition of a common ancestral soil, the organization of the work on a legal basis, the founding of Jewish societies of agriculture, industry and commerce on the Mosaic, i.e., social principles, these are the foundations on which Oriental Jewry will rise again, and in its rise, will rekindle the glimmering fire of the old Jewish patriotism and light the way to a new life for the Jewry of the entire world. On the common ground of Jewish patriotism, all Jewish classes will meet, orthodox and progressive, rich and poor. They will recognize themselves as the descendants of those heroes who fought the mightiest and the most civilized nations of antiquity: the Egyptians, Assyrians, Greeks, and Romans, and succeeded in carrying on their struggle to the very end of the ancient world, which they alone survived. They will look upon themselves as children of that race which, unlike any other people of history, has suffered a two thousand year martyrdom, and which has always carried aloft the banner of nationality, namely, the Book of the Law.

I will have to interrupt our correspondence for the present, in order to quote to you from a Hebrew work recently published by an extremely pious scholar. The author, after thoroughly discussion the question of Jewish Nationalism from a Talmudic point of view, arrives at the same results that the Christian Frenchman reached in his brochure *A new Oriental Question,* and to which I heartily subscribe in all detail. I will city to you a few lines from this work, as I have done in the case of the French pamphlet. The author closes his work with the following words:

"Even if the time of Grace has not yet come, when we should think of erecting an altar to the Lord in Zion, even if we cannot expect to win the consent of the Sultan, the following proposal is still practical, especially at a time when under God's Providence, there have arisen in Israel a number of men who possess great political influence or rule, by virtue of their wealth, men like Montefiore, Albert Cohn, Rothschild, Fould, and others. These men are Jewish princes such as the Jewish people has not had since the dispersion. These should organize a Society for the colonization of Palestine, a *Chebra Eretz Nosheveth.* A large number of the rich and respected Jews of all parts of the world will undoubtedly join them. The program of the organization may include the following activities:

a. First, it should raise a fund sufficient to buy as many towns, fields and vineyards in the Holy Land as possible. Let the desert turn into the Lebanon and the hilly places to fruit-bearing plains, and the desert shall again blossom like a lily and bring forth fruit like the field blessed by God. And thus, gradually, the Society will acquire hills, and dales, and fields, and villages, which it will in time rent out to the colonists.

b. Jews from all parts of the world, and especially from Russia, Poland and Germany, should be brought over by the Society and be settled in Palestine. Those who are not practical farmers should be taught under the direction of experienced teachers, employed by the Company. But those who are acquainted with agriculture should be granted a tract of land free of rent for a time, until they are able to pay the company a fixed amount of rent. During the first years, the company should, in addition, make loans of money to the indigent farmers until such time as the land begins to yield its harvests.

c. Thirdly, a police system must be established by this Society, to protect the colonists from the attacks of the Bedouins, and to maintain law and order in the land in general.

d. Finally, there should be opened under the auspices of the Society an agricultural school where Jewish youths could receive an adequate preparation for the life of a Palestinian farmer. This school, in which also other sciences will be taught and a knowledge of the Jewish religion imparted, can be established either in Palestine or in any of the lands of the exile; but it must be located in a land where wine and oil and other fruits of the Holy Land are raised, so that the pupils of the school may be prepared to undertake agriculture in Palestine.

God in his grace will then support us, and we will, though small in our beginning, continually grow and come more and more into the possession of the Holy Land, as the prophet foresaw. We, however, must make the beginning, as I have proved by numerous citations from Talmud and Midrash."

Thus far Rabbi Kalisher, of Thorn.

Was I not right when I praised the practical sense of our people to you and asserted that pious Jews will join hands with the enlightened on the common ground of Jewish Nationalism? From another source we are told, that last December a meeting was held in Australia, which was attended by many Christian and Jewish notables, and where resolutions similar in spirit to the conclusions arrived at by our Frenchman and the learned rabbi were proposed to a large assembly and unanimously adopted.[1]

And thus not only Jews of different lands and different grades of education, but most Christian denominations and different peoples concur in the desire to restore our people to its national heritage. And the most remarkable thing about it is that they all agree on the same means to the end. If I still needed corroboration for the convictions arrived at after years of study and life experience, I should find it in the concurring opinions of different men and peoples, who having started from different points of view, have arrived at the same results. I already foresee the organization of the Society proposed by the pious Jewish patriot, and its ultimate settling of the Holy Land with Jewish colonists under the protection of the Western civilized nations. When the Jewish situation in Palestine is once for all adjusted under the protection of the law, and on the foundation of labor, there will arise in the Holy Land, as in Germany and other European countries, universities conducted by able scholars whose spirit will not conflict with but harmonize with the ancient Jewish national religion.

The faithful watchmen of the sacred grave of our nationality, in spite of their poverty, do not wish to accept help which may injure the ancient Jewish cult, and our Western philanthropists continue to complain that "you cannot do anything with these people." Indeed, the lack of system and the wrong plans of the philanthropists lead to no results; they bring only discord. But at least, do not blame those who would rather die in misery in the Holy Land than give up some precepts of their ancient religion. Blame your ignorance of the needs of Jewry, blame the spirit of the times, when you can show so little success in all your undertakings, whether in the Orient or the Occident.

The rigid crust of orthodox Jewry will melt when the spark of Jewish patriotism, now smoldering under it, is kindled into a sacred fire which will herald the coming of the spring and the resurrection of our nation to a new life. On the other hand, Occidental Judaism is surrounded by an almost undissolvable crust, composed of the dead residue of the first manifestation of the modern spirit, from the inorganic chalk deposit of an extinct rationalistic enlightenment. This crust will not be melted by the fire of Jewish patriotism; it can only be broken by an external pressure under the weight of which everything which has no future must give up its existence. In contradistinction to orthodoxy, which cannot be destroyed by an external force without at the same time endangering the embryo of Jewish Nationalism that slumbers within it, the hard covering that surrounds the hearts of our cultured Jews will be Shattered only by a blow from without, one that world events are already preparing; and which will probably fall in the near future. The old framework of European Society, battered so often by the storms of revolution, is cracking and groaning on all sides. It can no longer stand a storm. Those who stand between revolution and reaction, the mediators, who have an appointed purpose to push modern Society on its path of progress, will after society becomes strong and progressive, be swallowed up by it. The nurses of progress, who would undertake to teach the Creator himself wisdom, prudence and economy; those carriers of culture, the saviors of Society, the speculators in politics, philosophy and religion, will not survive the last storm. And along with the other nurses of progress our Jewish reformers will also close their ephemeral existence. On the other hand, the Jewish people, along with other historical nations will, after this last catastrophe, the approach of which is attested by unmistakable signs of the times, receive its full rights as a people.

"Remember the days of old,
Consider the years of many generations;

[1]See Note X at end of book.

Ask thy father and he will tell thee,
Thy elders and they will inform thee,
When the Most High divided to the nations their inheritance,
When he separated the sons of Adam,
He set the bounds of the peoples
According to the number of the Children of Israel."[2]

Just as after the last catastrophe of organic life, when the historical races came into the world's arena, there came their division into tribes, and the position and rôle of the latter was determined, so after the last catastrophe in social life, when the spirit of humanity shall have reached its maturity, will our people, with the other historical people, find its legitimate place in universal history.

[2]Deut. xxxii, 7-8.

EPILOGUE

I. HELLENES AND HEBREWS

The spiritual views of a man, of whatever religion or race, are the products of his particular environment. But the roots of these conceptions, as well as those of social life in general, lie in the great web of organic life with which the social life is closely and inseparably connected; just as organic life itself is connected with the next life sphere, the cosmic.

There is no absolute line of demarcation between these three life spheres, just as there is no difference between the material and the spiritual life. The three life spheres do, however, form sharply defined grades or epochs within the unified and indivisible universal life. And just as in each individual life sphere, so also in the totality of the universal life, every step toward a higher grade of life must have its antecedents in the lower grade. Compared with the higher order of life, the organic, the cosmic life sphere appears lifeless, especially on the border line which leads from the life of the cosmic bodies to that of the organisms. Here, on the surface of the already cooled-off and stiffened cosmic bodies, we see only the dead residue of the cosmic life sphere, out of which the higher organic life sphere developed. But if we observe the life of the cosmic sphere where it is still being generated and developed in universal space, we cannot deny to it attributes of the divine life—the life that is so beautifully described in our literature in the Words: "Last in creation, first in thought." The remarkable phenomena which were observed in the modern period, such as the splitting and other changes going on in the double comets of Bielasch and Liais, the solidifying of the cosmic dust, its assumption of the spheroid form and spiral movement, and finally the grouping of these bodies into sidereal and planetary systems, these and other similar phenomena are life processes which can be as little explained by an external and one-sided mechanical gravitation theory, as the process of the division of the embryonic cell or the grouping of the organs in an organism.

Similarly, the human, the social life sphere, rises infinitely higher than the organic, but is in nowise different from it; just as organic life does not differ essentially from the cosmic. Here, also, we meet, on the border-line which leads from the organic into the social life sphere, the natural organic race which, compared with the higher humanitarian life, is spiritless. But in spite of this appearance of spiritlessness, the race is the root of the social life sphere, just as the cosmic bodies were the soil out of which the organisms grew.

Social life is, first of all, a product of the life of definite races, composed of different folk-tribes, each of which has formed its life course in a typical way. In the course of historical development, the typical views of life of the various races came in conflict with one another. From the friction of those antithetical forces were generated the first sparks of the spirit, which contain the germs, out of which higher and more harmonious forms of life will spring forth.

The unity of the human genus is a conception developed in the course of ages through historical activity, and not an original, natural idea, inherent in the human soul. It is not an immediate datum of organic life, but a product of the social historical development process. It has the variety of the primitive racial tribes as its antecedent, their struggle as its conditions, and their final harmonious cooperation as its aim.

The thus conceived unity of mankind presupposes a plan of the history of humanity, namely, that the multiple phenomena of social life will finally unite and cooperate in a not less harmonious manner than the varied and different phenomena of organic and cosmic life. This unified, divine plan of history is, at present, apparently in its last stage of historical development. But in antiquity, when the nations were still in the grip of natural life, it was only one people, the people of Israel, which, thanks to its particular genius, was able to perceive the workings of the divine plan in the history of humanity, as well as in the organic and cosmic spheres of life.

If we consider the plan of history, as mapped out in the sacred Scriptures of the Jews, without prejudice, we shall see in it, not only the conception of the unity of mankind, but also the unity of all life, cosmic, organic and social. Our sacred Scriptures presuppose the unity of God, in spite of the apparent variety which the word presents, and the unity of the human genus, notwithstanding the differences of races; because the total plan of the history of the world seems to have been always present to the spirit of the Jewish people, from the beginning of its history. The entire literature of the Jews is to be conceived only from this genetic point of view. Judaism is a historical religion, a historical cult, in contradistinction to Paganism, which is a natural cult.

The revelation of the Jewish spirit, which was an isolated phenomenon at the dawn of the history of humanity, would have been inexplicable and would appear supernatural, were it not for the fact that there existed originally different tribes, with typically individual mental qualities, which had evolved fundamentally different views long before the revelation of the Jewish spirit. This same remarkable manifestation of individuality is met in the divergent languages of primitive peoples. Primitive religions and primitive languages are, as Renan has rightly observed, race creations; though he himself had hardly any conception of the importance of the ancient Jewish historical religion. History corroborates the story of anthropology, that there were originally different human races and tribes.[1]

If the various races and peoples that still exist were not primal, then, in such places as Western Asia, Northern Africa and Europe, where peoples have lived together for thousands of years, commingling through intermarriage and influenced by common climatic conditions, there should have been produced a type, in which there is no trace of their foregone ancestors. But all human races and tribal types, known to us either from historical monuments, or who still live to-day in their primitive homes, in spite of climatic and cultural influences, have reproduced their original types in such a way that the anthropologist can tell, at a glance, the different types of humanity, according to their physiological and psychical characteristics. The most ancient Egyptian monuments depict negroes as well as Indo-Germanic and Semitic types, races which have lived from time immemorial in the same land and which were likewise scattered in different countries and climates, yet their primal types have not undergone any perceptible changes.

The languages of those nations with whom our civilization originated belong to two primal races, the Indo-Germanic and the Semitic. The ancient culture of the former reached its culminating point in Greece; of the later, in Judæa. In these two countries the typical antithesis between the Indo-Germanic and Semitic races reached its highest point, and the fundamental differences in the views of life of these two races were expressed in the classical works of the Hellenes and Hebrews. We see, from those works, that the former viewed life as a multiplicity and the latter as a unity; the one, looked upon the world as eternal *being,* the other, as eternal *becoming.* The spirit of the

---

[1] In this, as well as in the subsequent passage, Hess endeavors to prove his objection ot the doctrine of monogenism, the theory that there was originally only one race and that the differences between the races are only secondary, acquired through the influence of environment. Hess believes that the various races existing to-day are not modifications of one mother-race, but are primal and essentially different races; their characteristics are not acquired, but inherent. He does not, however, explain how these original and primal races suddenly came into existence. For a more detailed discussion of this question, see Hote VII and Introduction.— *Translator.*

one expressed itself in terms of space, that of the other, in terms of time. In the expression of the Greek spirit, there is the underlying idea of a perfectly created world; the Hebrew spirit, on the other hand, is permeated with the invisible energy of becoming, and the world, according to it, is governed by a principle which will begin its workday in social life, when it has arrived at a standstill in the world of Nature. The classical representatives of the natural Sabbath no longer exist as a people, and the God of history has dispersed his people, which foresaw the historical Sabbath, among the nations. But the two primal types of spirit, which no longer have classical nations as their representatives, have still many such individuals among civilized nations. The two giants of German literature, Goethe and Schiller, are the German representatives of the two types of genius—the Greek and the Hebrew of the natural and historical Sabbath. And when Heine divides all men into Hellenists and Nazarenes, he designates, unconsciously, these two types of spirit. Modern Jews, like the Indo-Germanic nations, have in Heine and "Börne" their representatives of these two types of cultural life.[2]

After the antithesis of the two spiritual tendencies reached its culminating points in two historical peoples, the conciliation of these two points of view became the task of the civilized nations.

The first attempt at a reconciliation of the two types of civilization was made by Christianity, followed by that of Islam, which contested the right to dominion of the former, in Asia, Africa and even in a part of Europe itself, namely, in Spain. Just as the process of conciliation started from the contact of the Hellenic and Jewish cultures, in the ancient Jewish fatherland, so in the meeting of Arabic, Jewish and European cultures in Spain, the second fatherland of the Jews, the final mediation process between the two types of universal history had its origin. But the spiritual spark which arose out of the friction of the two tendencies, and which became the germ of a higher harmonious tendency in which the natural racial antitheses of the historical peoples will ultimately find their reconciliation, this social light germ, the new revelation, was generated by the Jewish genius.

When pagan Rome brought the ancient Hellenic and Jewish cultural life to an end; there arose, from the ruins of the latter, a new view of the world; and when Christian Rome struck the mortal blow at the Arabic and Jewish cultural life in Spain, there arose again, in the mind of a Jew, from the ruins of the latter, the modern world view. Spinoza was a descendant of the Spanish Jews, who fled to Holland in order to escape the "holy" Inquisition.

II. CHRIST AND SPINOZA

From Judaism, permeated with the scientific spirit, Christianity will receive full justice and its importance will be properly estimated. The Jewish historian no longer finds it necessary to assume an attitude of fanaticism toward it. Graetz, in the third volume of his history, has shown how one can be a loyal Jew and at the same time an objective judge of that phenomenon which has been a source of persecution to the Jews for the last eighteen hundred years. A few quotations from that writer will show with what freedom of spirit and objectivity a Jewish historian, not a reformer, has characterized Christianity and its founder.

"While Judæa was still trembling," says our Jewish historian, "lest the procurator Pontius Pilate strike a blow at the population, which might result in a rising in arms and great suffering, a strange event occurred. It was so small in its beginning that

---

[2]"Natural Sabbath" and "Historical Sabbath" are used "by Hess as symbolic expressions; the former view looks upon the world as an accomplished thing, the latter, only a becoming, i.e., a continuous creation. The one is the expression of the Hellenic spirit, the other that of the Hebrew.—*Translator.*

people scarcely noticed it, but gradually, through the force of circumstances, it assumed such proportions that it turned the history of the world into new paths... Israel was now to commence his mission in earnest; he was to become the teacher of nations."[3]

"It was due to the strange movement which arose under the governorship of Pilate, that the teachings of Judaism won the sympathy of the heathen world. But this new form of Judaism, changed by foreign elements, became estranged from and antagonistic to the source from which it sprang. Judaism could hardly rejoice at her offspring, which soon turned coldly from her and struck out into strange, divergent paths. If Judaism does not wish to strip off its ancient individuality and become disloyal to its own convictions, it must continue its existence in opposition to the religion to which she gave birth. This new movement, this old doctrine in a new garb, or rather Essenism intermingled with foreign elements, is Christianity, whose advent and early development belong to the Judæan history of this epoch."

"As regards Jesus himself," says Graetz, "on account of his Galilean origin, he could not have stood high in that knowledge of the Law which through the schools of Shammai and Hillel had become prevalent in Judæa. His small stock of learning and his corrupt half-Aramaic language pointed unmistakably to his birthplace in Galilee. His deficiency in knowledge, however, was compensated by his intensely sympathetic character. Earnestness and moral purity were his undeniable attributes; they stand out in all the authentic accounts of his life that have reached us, and appear even in those garbled teachings which his followers placed in his mouth. The gentle disposition and the humility of Jesus remind one of Hillel, whom he seems to have taken as his model, and whose golden rule, "What you wish not to be done to yourself, do not do unto others," he adopted as the starting-point of his moral code. Like Hillel, Jesus looked upon promotion of peace and the forgiveness of injuries as the highest forms of virtue. His whole being was permeated by that deeper religiousness which consecrates to God not only the hour of prayer, a day of penitence, and longer or shorter periods of devotional exercise, but every step in the journey of life, which turns every aspiration of the soul toward Him, subjects everything to His will, and with childlike trust, commits everything to His keeping. He was filled with that tender, brotherly love which Judaism teaches should be manifested even to an enemy. Certainly no curse against his enemies escaped his lips, and his enthusiastic admirers have done him an injustice when they placed in his mouth a curse or even unfriendly words against his own mother. He reached the ideal of the passive virtues which the Pharisees inculcated: "Be of the oppressed and not of the oppressors; receive abuse and return it not; let the motive of all your actions be the love of God, and rejoice in suffering."[4]

"Jesus must, from the idiosyncrasies of his nature, have been powerfully attracted by the Essenes, who led a contemplative life apart from the world and its vanities. When John, the Baptist—or more correctly, the Essene,—invited all to come to receive baptism in the Jordan, to repent and prepare for the Kingdom of Heaven, Jesus hastened to obey the call and was baptized by him. Although it cannot be proved that Jesus was formally admitted into the order of the Essenes, much of his life and work can only be explained on the supposition that he had adopted their fundamental principles. Like the Essenes, Jesus highly esteemed self-inflicted poverty, and despised the mammon of riches... Community of goods, a peculiar doctrine of the Essenes, was

---

[3] *Geschichte der Juden,* 2nd edition, Vol. III, Ch. XI, p. 216. The chapter, from which we cite only a few fragments, gives to the history of the development of Christianity, a new historical viewpoint and supplies it with new sources. See also Vol. IV, Chapter V, VIII, IX, and notes.

[4] Sabbath, 88b; Yoma, 23a; Gittin, 36b. The style of the sayings indicates that they were originally a part of an ancient *Baraitha.*

not only approved, but positively enjoined by Jesus, for his close disciples had a common purse and shared their goods. Like the Essenes, he reprobated every form of oath. "Swear not at all," taught Jesus, "neither by heaven nor by the earth, nor by your head, but let your yea be yea, and your nay be nay" (James v. 12). Miraculous cures said to have been performed by him, such as exorcism of demons from those who believed themselves to be possessed, were often made by the Essenes. It was, therefore, not considered a special miracle that Jesus could do the same thing. We can also infer from the life that his friends led, that the founder of the sect embraced Essenism. Of his brother James, it is said, with all certainty that he led the life of an Essene, for he did not drink wine nor eat meat nor use oil, and always dressed in linen. But it would seem that Jesus adopted only the essential traits of Essenism, such as the predilection for poverty, the contempt for riches and property, the community of goods, celibacy, the fear of pronouncing an oath and the ability to exert a curative influence upon maniacs. The unimportant practices, such as the observance of strict levitical purity, the frequent taking of baths and the wearing of linen robes, he dropped. Even baptism did not play an important rôle with him, for we do not find it emphasized either in the stories told about him or in the sayings attributed to him."

"After John had been imprisoned by Herod Antipas in the fortress of Macharus, Jesus thought simply of continuing his master's work. Like John, he preached "Repent, for the Kingdom of Heaven is at hand,"[5] without perhaps having then a suspicion of the part he was afterward to play in that Kingdom of Heaven. Jesus apparently felt that if his appeal was not to be lost in the desert, like that of the Baptist, but bring forth lasting results, it must not be addressed to the whole nation, but to a particular class of the Jews. The middle classes, inhabitants of towns of greater or lesser importance, were not wanting in godliness, piety and morality, and consequently a call to them to repent and forsake their sins would have been meaningless. The declaration made to Jesus by the young man who was seeking the way of eternal life, 'From my youth I have kept the laws of God; I have not committed murder or adultery, nor have I stolen or borne false witness; I have honored my father and loved my neighbor as myself,'[6] might have been made by the greater number of the middle-class Jews of that time. The description of the later writers of the corruption of the Jews and of the hypocrisy of the Pharisees, in the time of Jesus, is pure fiction. The disciples of Shammai and Hillel, the followers of the zealot Judas, the bitter foes of the Herodians and of Rome, were not morally sick and were not in need of a physician. They were ever ready for self-sacrifice and Jesus wisely refrained from turning to them. Still less was he inclined to attempt to reform the rich, the friends of the Romans and the Herodians. From these, the yearning of the simple, unlearned moralist and preacher, his reproof of their pride, their venality and inconstancy, would only have elicited mockery and derision. Jesus therefore determined to seek out those who did not belong to or had been expelled from the Jewish community. There were in Judæa at the time many who had no conception of the wholesome truths of Judaism, of its laws, its history and its future. They were publicans and tax-gatherers who were shunned by the patriots, as promoters of Roman interests, who turned their backs upon the Law, and led a wild life, heedless alike of the past and of the future. There were also poor, ignorant handicraftsmen and menials (*Am-haaretz*), who were seldom able to visit the capital, or listen to teachings which, indeed, they would probably not have understood. It was not for them that Sinai had flamed or the prophets had uttered their cry of warning; for the teachers of the Law, more intent upon expounding doctrines than upon reforming their hearers, failed to make the Law and the prophets intelligible to those

[5]Matthew iv, 12. In the parallel passage, Mark i, 15, there are added to the above the rather suspicious words: "and believe the gospel." The term *Evangelion* is of post-Pauline origin and could hardly have been used by Jesus.
[6]Matthew, xix, 16-20, and parallel passages.

85

classes, and consequently did not draw them into their fold. It was to these classes that Jesus turned, to snatch them out of their torpor, their ignorance and their ungodliness. He felt that he was called to save the 'lost sheep of the house of Israel.' 'They that be whole need not a physician, but they that are sick.'[7]

"Jesus, however, by word and example, raised the sinner and publican, and filled the hearts of those poor, neglected people with the love of God, transforming them into dutiful children of their heavenly Father. He animated them with his own piety and fervor and improved their conduct by the hope he gave them of being able to enter the Kingdom of Heaven. Above all things, he taught his male and female disciples the Essene virtues of self-abnegation and humility, of the contempt for riches, of charity and the love of peace. He bade them become sinless as little children, and declared they must be as if born again, if they would become members of the approaching Messianic Kingdom. The law of brotherly love and forbearance he carried to the extent of self-immolation. 'If one smite thee on one cheek, turn to him the other also; and if one sue thee at law and take away thy coat, let him have thy cloak also.' He taught the poor that they should not take heed for meat or drink or raiment, but pointed to the birds of the air and the lilies of the field that were fed and clothed, yet 'they toil not neither do they spin': He taught the rich how to distribute alms—'Let not thy left hand know what thy right hand doeth.' He admonished the hypocrite, and bade him pray in the secrecy of his closet, placing before him a short form of prayer—'Our Father,' which may possibly have been in use among the Essenes.

"Jesus made no attack upon Judaism itself. He had no idea of becoming the reformer of Jewish doctrine or the propounder of a new Law. He sought merely to redeem the sinner, to call him to a good and holy life and to make him worthy of participation in the approaching Messianic time. He insisted upon the unity of God, and was far from attempting to change in the slightest degree the Jewish conception of the Deity. To the question once put to him by an expounder of the law, 'What is the essence of Judaism?' he replied, 'Hear, O Israel, our God is one,' and 'Thou shalt love thy neighbor as thyself';—these are the chief commandments. When a man approached him with the words: 'Good Master;' Jesus remarked: 'Call me not good, there is none good but One, that is, my Father in Heaven': His disciples, who remained true to Judaism, promulgated the declaration of their master 'I have not come to destroy but to fulfill till heaven and earth pass, one jot or one tittle shall in nowise pass from the Law till all be fulfilled.'[8]

He must have kept the Sabbath holy, for those of his followers who were attached to Judaism strictly observed the Sabbath, which they would not have done had their master disregarded it. It was only the Shammaitic strictness in the observance of the Sabbath which forbade even the healing of the sick on that day, that Jesus protested against, declaring that it was lawful to do good on the Sabbath. Jesus made no objection to the existing custom of sacrifice, he merely demanded—and in this the Pharisees agreed with him—that reconciliation with one's fellow-man should precede any act of atonement.[9] He did not even oppose fasting when practiced without ostentation or hypocrisy. He was so completely Jewish, that he shared the narrow views of his time, and, like the Jews of the period, thoroughly despised the heathen world, which included the Roman oppressors and their followers, the Oriental Greeks

---

[7]Matthew ix, 12; x, 5; xv, 24; xviii, 11-14, and parallel passages.
[8]Matthew v, 17-19. Cf. The Epistle of James, x, 12. The fact that the extreme antinomist Mark formulates the saying in the opposite sense, namely, "I have come to abrogate the Law," proves the authenticity of the original form as quoted in the two synoptic Gospels. We find in the Talmud (Sabbath, 116b) the same saying in its gospel form: "And it is written in it (i.e. in the Gospel): 'I have not come to abrogate any law of Moses or to add anything to it.'"
[9]Cf. the last Mishnah of Yoma.

and Syrians. One must not throw holy things to the dogs, he taught, nor cast pearls before swine, lest they trample them under their feet and urn again and rend you. When a Canaanite or a Syrian Greek woman from Phoenician implored him to heal her possessed daughter, he replied harshly, "I was sent only to the lost sheep of the house of Israel and it is not right to take the bread away from the mouth of the children and cast it to the dogs." To his disciples he repeatedly spoke: Do not follow in the paths of the heathens and do not enter the cities of the Samaritans. While Jesus thus confined himself to the bounds of Judaism, he had no intention to proclaim a new revelation or to originate a new covenant,[10] but limited himself to the task of sowing the seeds of religion and morality in such hearts as had heretofore been barren of it. Jesus did not teach the immortality of the soul, in the sense of a continued existence of the soul after its liberation from the body and its sojourning in the abode of heaven, but emphasized the resurrection of the body at a definite time,[11] in accordance with the teachings of Judaism current in his day. The resurrection of the just and pious was, according to him, to take place on earth, and as the beginning of the inauguration of a new order of things, the future world (*Olom habba*), which he, like the Pharisees and Essenes, identified with the Messianic era and the initiation of the Kingdom of Heaven. He, like the Pharisees, threatened sinners with eternal punishment in a fiery pit (*Gehenna*).[12] The merit of Jesus consists in his efforts to impart inner force to the precepts of Judaism, in his upholding the Jewish doctrine of the Brotherhood of Man, in his insistence that moral laws be placed in the foreground, and in his endeavors to have them accepted by those who had hitherto been regarded as the lowest and most degraded of human beings.

His great design, the central point of all his thoughts, Jesus disclosed on one occasion to the most intimate circle of his disciples. He led them to a retired spot at the foot of Mount Hermon, near Cæsarea Philippi, where the Jordan rushes forth from mighty rocks, and in that remote solitude he revealed to them the hidden object of his thoughts. But he contrived his discourse in a way that it appeared to be his disciples, who at last elicited from him the revelation that he considered himself the expected Messiah. He asked his followers whom they thought him to be. Some replied that he was thought to be Elijah, the forerunner of the Messiah; others that he was the prophet whose advent Moses had predicted; upon which Jesus asked them, "But whom say ye that I am?" Simon Peter answered and said, "Thou art the Christ." Jesus praised Peter's discernment and admitted that he was the Messiah, but forbade his disciples to divulge the truth, or, for the present, from speaking about it at all.[13] Such was the mysteriously-veiled birth of Christianity. When, a few days later, the most trusted of his disciples, Simon Peter, and the two sons of Zebedee, James and John, timidly suggested that Elijah must precede the Messiah, Jesus replied that Elijah had already appeared, though unrecognized, in the person of the Baptist.[14] Had Jesus from the very commencement of his career nourished these thoughts in the depths of his soul, or had they first taken shape when the many followers he had gained seemed to make their realization possible? This is a puzzle which cannot be solved. Jesus never

[10]It is true that the Sermon on the Mount in Matthew, chs. v-vii, partly represents Jesus as one who wishes to oppose his teaching to the Law. But the authenticity of the Sermon itself is very doubtful. Mark does not record the Sermon on the Mount at all. Luke knows it only in part. We may, therefore, suspect it to be an interpolation in Matthew's groundwork. Finally, it is full of contradictions; here, the Law is praised and immediately afterward it is condemned. Is it possible that Jesus should have uttered such an untruthful statement in regard to the Law as "It is written, 'Hate thy enemy'?" (Ibid., v, 43). Only an enemy of the Law like Mark could have formulated it, he who established the famous antithesis between Judaism and Christianity and who did not always adhere to the truth.
[11]Matthew xxii, 23-32.
[12]Matthew v, 22.
[13]Matthew xvi, 13-20. In the Gospel of Mark (viii, 27-30), the story retains more of its originality. In Luke ix, 18, it is more or less confused.
[14]Matthew xvii, 10. iii.

publicly called himself the Messiah, but made use of other expressions which were doubtless current among the Essenes. He called himself "the Son of Man,"[15] (*Bar-Nash*), alluding probably to Daniel vii, "One like the son or man came with the clouds of heaven, and came to the Ancient of Days," a verse which, at that time, was made to point to the Messiah himself. There was yet another name which Jesus applied to himself[16] in his Messianic character—the mysterious words "Son of God," probably taken from the seventh verse of the second Psalm, "The Lord has said unto me, thou art my son, this day have I begotten thee," a verse which was in certain Jewish circles interpreted to refer to the Messiah.[17] Was this expression used by Jesus figuratively, or did he wish it to be taken in a literal sense? As far as we know, he never explained himself clearly on this subject, not even later, when it was on account of the meaning attached to these words that he was brought to trial. His followers afterward disagreed among themselves upon the matter, and the various ways in which they interpreted his words divided them into different sects among which a new form of idolatry unfolded itself.

Other appellations were employed by Jesus to designate his Messianic character, such as "Heavenly Bread" (*Manna*) and the "Bread of Life,"[18] expressions which were doubtless employed by the Essenes. He called followers "the salt of the earth."[19] How Jesus expected to fulfill the Messianic expectations, is nowhere indicated. It is only certain that he thought only of Israel, whom he expected to deliver, both from the burden of sin and the yoke of the Romans.[20] Of the pagan world, he thought as little, when considering himself the Messiah, as when he was only a disciple of John the Baptist. He probably pictured to himself the redemption of Israel in the following manner: that when the Jewish people, through love of God and man, through self-denial and the assumption of voluntary poverty, would rise, under his leadership, to a higher life, God, out of love to his people, would perform for them all sorts of miracles, such as the deliverance from the rule of the Romans, the return of the exiled tribes and final restoration of Israel to its former Davidic splendor.

When Jesus made himself known to his disciples as the Messiah, he enjoined upon them, as remarked already, to keep the revelation secret. Whether it was the fear of Herod Antipas, the slayer of the Baptist, that inspired this cautious measure, or whether he intended to wait until a larger circle of disciples gathered about him to reveal himself as the Messiah, cannot be ascertained. He consoled his disciples for the present silence imposed upon them, by the assurance that a time would come when "What I tell you in darkness, that speak ye in the light, and what ye hear in the ear, that preach ye upon the house tops." What occurred was contrary to what Jesus and his disciples expected, for as soon as it was known (the disciples having probably not kept the secret), that Jesus of Nazareth not only came to preach the Kingdom of Heaven, but proclaimed himself as the expected Messiah, public sentiment rose against him. He was asked to give proofs and signs that he was the Messiah, which he was not able to do, and he was thus forced constantly to evade the questions addressed to him. Many of his followers were vexed at his assuming the rôle of a Messiah, and left him. In order not to be discredited in the eyes of his disciples, it was necessary that he should perform some miracle that would crown his work or seal it with his death. They expected, first, that he would appear in the capital at the time of the Passover

[15]Matthew, xvii, 10.
[16]Cf. Sanhedrin, 98a. There the Messiah is called by a hybrid name *Bar-Nefile*, a Greek word, meaning "son of the clouds." See also ibid., 96b.
[17]Sukka, 52a.
[18]John vi, 35, 41.
[19]Matthew v, 13-14, and parallel passages.
[20]Luke xxiv, 21.

Feast and there declare himself in the Temple, in the presence of all the people, as the Messiah. It is said that his own brothers entreated him to go to the capital, so that his disciples should at last see his great work. "For there is no man that doeth anything in secret and he himself seeketh to be known openly. If thou do these things, show thyself to the world." (John vii, 4.) And so Jesus was finally forced to enter upon the path of danger. How many years Jesus spent in Galilee is unknown; the Gospel sources seem to indicate that his residence there lasted only one year, so little did they know the actual events. According to later authorities, the time passed by Jesus in his native district was three years.[21]

He wished to prevent any misconception as to his desire to change the Law, and his ready reply to the Pharisee who asked what would be required of him if he became his disciple was, "If thou wilt enter into life, keep the commandments; sell what thou hast and give to the poor." When he passed Jericho and came near to the capital, he took up his abode near the walls of Jerusalem, in the village of Bethany, at the Mount of Olives, where the lepers, who were forced to avoid the city, had their settlement. He found shelter in the house of one of these outcasts by the name of Simon, who, together with his fellow-sufferers, became his followers. The other followers that he found at Bethany belonged also to the lower class, such as Lazarus and his sisters, Mary and Martha. The sources know only of one rich resident of Jerusalem, Joseph of Arimathea, who became a disciple of Jesus.

The account of Jesus' entry in Jerusalem as recorded in the Gospel is of a legendary character. It seems incredible that the people should one day have conducted him into the city in a triumphal march, and the following day have demanded his death. The one account, like the other, is pure invention, the first designed for the purpose of showing that the masses recognized him as the Messiah, the second, in order to throw the guilt of his execution upon the entire people of Israel. There is also little historical truth in the story that Jesus forced his way into the Temple, overthrew the tables of the money-changers, and drove out the dove-sellers from their stalls. Such extraordinary action would not have been passed over in silence by contemporary historians. Nor is it anywhere mentioned that money-changers and dove-sellers had their tables within the precincts of the Temple. We know, however, that the Temple management sold the necessary wine, birds, or oil to those who brought sacrifices.[22]

But it is just the most important facts in the life of Jesus, namely, the attitude which he assumed toward the people of Jerusalem, the Sanhedrin and the sects, the question whether he really declared himself publicly as the Messiah, and how the declaration was received by the people, which are enveloped by the Gospel writers in such an impenetrable veil of mystery, that one cannot fail to suspect the legendary character of the whole story. There undoubtedly existed strong prejudices against him among the people of the capital. The educated classes could hardly be expected to accept an unlearned Galilean as the Messiah. Such a supposition would have contradicted the age-long tradition, that the Messiah was to come from Bethlehem and be a descendant of the house of David. It is possible that the proverb, "Can any good thing come out of Nazareth?" originated at this time. Devout Jews, no doubt, took offence because he associated with sinners and publicans, eating and drinking with them. Even the disciples of John, the Essenes, were displeased.[23]

The Shammaites certainly objected to his healing of the sick on the Sabbath, and would not have hailed one, who, in their eyes, violated the Sabbath, as the Messiah.

[21] Irenaeus, *contra haereses,* ii, 38-39

[22] Shekalim, iv, 3; v, 4.

[23] Matthew xi, 2-9.

Neither could the Zealots expect much of Jesus, who did not inspire his followers with hatred toward the oppressors, the Romans, but, on the contrary, preached non-resistance and willing submission to the Roman authorities as expressed in his saying: "Render, therefore, unto Cesar the things which are Cesar's, and unto God, the things which are God's" (Matthew xxii, 21). All these circumstances, which could by no means be reconciled with the traditional conception of the Messiah, caused the higher and the learned classes to assume an indifferent attitude toward him, and consequently he could not have been received in Jerusalem with any marked degree of enthusiasm. All these objections, however, afforded no ground for any legal accusation against him. Freedom of thought and difference of opinion had, owing to the frequent debates between the schools of Shammai and Hillel, become a firmly established right, and one would hardly be prosecuted because of a difference in a religious opinion, provided, however, that he did not openly violate any of the authoritative laws or reject the accepted conception of God. It was just in this regard that Jesus laid himself open to accusation. The report had spread that Jesus had called himself the Son of God, an appellation which, if taken literally, undermines the very essential religious conceptions of Judaism; so that the representatives of the religion could not afford to pass the incident over in silence. But how was it possible for the tribunal to ascertain whether Jesus really used the expression, or what meaning he attached to the words? How could they discover the secret of his sect? It was necessary for this purpose to find a traitor from among his disciples. Such a man was found in Judas Iscariot, who, incited by greed, delivered to the tribunal, we are told, the man whom he heretofore had revered as the Messiah. A Jewish source, of ancient origin and apparently trustworthy, seems to place in the true light the use made of this traitor. The Court required, in order to arraign Jesus either as a false prophet or as a seducer of the people (*Mesith*), the evidence of two witnesses, who had heard him call himself by the name "Son of God." Judas was therefore required to induce him to speak on the subject, so that the two witnesses, concealed nearby, should be able to hear every word. This extraordinary process of obtaining testimony against a suspected person was employed only in one case, namely, when a person was suspected of being a seducer of the people.[24]

According to the Christian sources, Judas' act of treachery consisted in this: that he pointed Jesus out to his accusers by giving him a kiss of homage while surrounded by his disciples and the masses. It is strange, however, that such a stratagem should be employed to identify a man who, according to the self-same accounts, had entered Jerusalem in triumphal procession and preached openly in the Temple! As soon as Jesus was seized by the soldiers, almost all of his disciples left him and sought safety in flight; Simon Peter was the only one who remained. At daybreak, on the 14th of Nissan; namely, on the eve of the Feast of Unleavened Bread, Jesus was brought before the Sanhedrin. It seems that the tribunal, before which he was brought to trial, was not the great Sanhedrin, but the smaller one, composed of twenty-three members, for the one who presided at the trial was not the President of the Sanhedrin, a member of the house of Hillel, but Joseph Caiaphas, the High Priest. The purpose of the trial was to determine whether Jesus really considered himself to be the Son of God, as the

---

[24]Both sources, the *Babylonian Talmud,* Sanhedrin, 67a (in the uncensored Amsterdam edition of 1645), and the Jerushalmi Palestinan Talmud Sanhedrin, vii, 16, relate that this special procedure of concealing witnesses was employed against Jesus. The first says: "And this procedure," alluding to what was mentioned before, "was followed in regard to Ben Satda, at Lud, and they hanged him on the day before Passover." The latter says: "Thus they did to Ben Satda at Lud. They concealed two witness and then they brought him to court and stoned him." The identification of Ben Satda and Jesus is assumed by the Talmud to be certain. The meaning of the word Satda, is not known. The etymological derivation which the Talmud gives *in loco,* as well as in Sabbath, 104b (uncensored edition), is rather odd. If we take into consideration the fact that during the Second Temple trials of seducers occurred very seldom or probably not at all, we are inclined to believe that the *halachah* in the above-quoted Mishnah and the Baraitha are the only authentic sources in the Talmud concerning Jesus.

witnesses had testified. It is rather unbelievable that he was tried, as the Gospels relate (Matt. xxvi, 61), because he was supposed to have boasted that he was able to destroy the Temple and build it up again in three days. Such an assertion, if really made by him, could not have been the object of an arraignment. The accusation doubtless pointed to the sin of blasphemy (*Gidduf-blasphemia*), and to the supposed affirmation of Jesus that he was the Son of God.[25] To the direct question as to that point, Jesus gave no answer and remained silent. When the President repeated the question and asked him if he were the Son of God, he answered, "Thou hast said it,"[26] and added, "Hereafter shall ye see the Son of Man sitting on the right hand of power and coming in the clouds of heaven" (Matt. xxvi, 24). On hearing this assertion, the judges concluded that he believed himself to be the Son of God. The High Priest rent his garments, and the Court condemned him to death as a blasphemer.[27] From the accounts of the Christian sources, we cannot infer that according to the existing penal laws, the judges had pronounced an unjust sentence against him. The evidence was against him. The Sanhedrin received the sanction of the sentence, or rather the permission to carry out the execution from Pontius Pilate, the Procurator, who happened then to be in Jerusalem.

Pilate, before whom Jesus was brought, asked him about the political side of his activity, whether he, as Messiah, had also declared himself King of the Jews, and when Jesus gave the ambiguous answer, "Thou hast said it," Pilate confirmed the sentence.[28] The story reported in the Gospels that Pilate had found him innocent but that the Jews had insistently clamored for his death is legendary.[29] When Jesus was scoffed at, and obliged to wear the crown of thorns in ironical allusion to the Messianic and royal dignity he had assumed, it was not the Jews who inflicted the indignities upon him, but the Roman soldiers, who sought through him to deride the Jewish nation. The Jewish judges manifested so little personal animosity toward Jesus that they gave him, as they gave to every other criminal, the cup of wine mixed with frankincense, in order to render him insensible to pains of death.[30] According to the then existing penal laws, a blasphemer was first to be stoned and after his death, to be hanged for a short time on a tree.[31] Jesus was executed in this manner. But the Christian sources would have us believe that he was crucified at nine in the morning, and that his torture lasted six

[25] Matthew xxvi, 63. It is rather strange that the Gospels state that the witnesses who testified against Jesus had given false testimony, while the Gospels themselves describe Jesus as repeatedly asserting that he was the Son of God, and this was just what the witnesses accused him of.

[26] The Gospel writers themselves did not know how Jesus answered the questions directed at him by the Court. According to Matthew xxvi, 64, the answer was: "Thou hast said it," which may mean, "yes," as well as "no." According to Luke xxii, 69, the answer was: "Ye say that I am," and according to Mark xiv, 69, his answer was: "I am he." According to John, Jesus confessed to the charge and pointed to his public activity—a rather suspicious move.

[27] The three Synoptic Gospels all agree that the Court condemned him on the charge of blasphemy. The fact that the President rent his garments, Matthew xxvi, 65; Mark xiv, 63-65, testifies to it, for the Sanhedrin, ch. vii, Mishnas, 10-11, requires such action on hearing the name of God blasphemed. Even John xix, 7, says that Jesus was condemned according to law, for he had declared himself as the Son of God.

[28] Three Synoptic Gospels, Matthew xxvii, 11; Mark xv, 2; Luke xxii, 3, report Jesus' answer to Pilate as the same he gave to the High Priest: "Thou hast said it," which is ambiguous. John xviii, 34f, makes him deny the assertion by asking Pilate a counter question, "Sayst thou this thing of thyself or did other tell it to thee of me?" and adding to it the declaration, "My kingdom is not of this world."

[29] Only Matthew xxvii, 24, reports that Pilate poured water on Jesus' hands as a sign of his innocence and that the dream of Pilate's wife was the cause of his believing Jesus guiltless. But the washing of the hands was a Jewish custom, prescribed in the case of a man found murdered and the perpetrator of the crime not having been discovered. Hence Pilate, as a Roman general, could not have employed it. Tightly have Kortlin and Hilgenfeld observed that this passage must have been inserted by a later follower of Paul, who wanted to demonstrate that the pagan Pilate and his wife were more favorably inclined toward Jesus than the Jews.

[30] Matthew xxvii, 24, and parallel passages. This cup of worwood wine was prescribed by the Law as an act of mercy. (Ebel Rabbatai or Semachoth, ch. xi, 9; Sanhedrin, 43a.) In the Gospels, however, it is described as an act of cruelty against Jesus. The Gospels also differ in regard to the liquid in question. Mark says, in agreement with the Talmud, that it consisted of wine and myrrh or frankincense. Matthew believes it to have been vingar and gall. The other writers do not mention the incident at all.

91

hours, until three in the afternoon, when he expired. His last words were a quotation from the Psalms, in the Aramaic dialect: "My God, my God, why hast thou forsaken me" ("Eli, eli, lama shebakhtani")? The Roman soldiers placed, in mockery, the following inscription upon the cross: "Jesus of Nazareth, King of the Jews." The crucifixion and the burial of the body probably took place outside of the town, on a spot by the name of Golgotha, the place of the skulls, reserved for the burial of condemned criminals. How great was the woe caused by that execution! It was the indirect cause of innumerable deaths and interminable suffering among millions of the sons of his people. Millions of broken hearts and tragic fates have not yet atoned for his death. He is the only mortal of whom it can be truthfully said that he influenced the world more by his death than by his life. Golgotha, the place of skulls, became for a great part of humanity, a new Sinai.[32]

The Jewish historian, in continuing his narrative, shows how, as a result of the Pauline trend of thought, which inclined toward the pagan view of life, there arose, already in the primitive Church, sects and difference of opinion, traces of which are to be recognized in the Gospel writings, the most ancient of which was composed, as late as the time of Bar Kochba (132-133). In order to conquer the pagan world, the daughter of Judaism was forced to make greater concessions to paganism than the latter made to Judaism.

Christianity represents a departure from the classical essence of both Judaism and Paganism. The Jewish view of the world was, and is, that the universe is a sacred creation of one Supreme Being. To Paganism, in its typical classical form, which reached its culmination in the Greek spirit, the divine unity, present in the world, appeared only as a product of the harmonious combination of multiple and various universal forces. The creative essence of Judaism did not disappear with its created classical culture, because the Jewish creative genius did not exhaust itself in its creation. Classical Paganism, however, saw its genius disappear with its culture, the roots of which lay only on the surface of life, and which were consequently swept away by the tide of barbarous tribes which flooded the ancient world during the closing period of antiquity. To the pagans, who saw the gradual disappearance of their own creative genius, along with the environment wherein it acted, it appeared, one day, that the divine harmony of the pluralistic world is no more divine and sacred but God-forsaken, and, finally, Paganism sought refuge in its opposite, the creative spirit of Judaism. On the other hand, only such Jews could satisfy the religious cravings of the Pagan world as had estranged themselves from their own world and were able to merge with the pagan environment so as to draw it along with themselves to the spirit which animated them—such Jews as did not look upon themselves as chosen children of a holy Being, but only as sinners and apostates. Thus there arose the double separation of the worldly element from the divine in Judaism on the one hand, and the divine from the worldly element in Paganism on the other; and as a result of the combination of a Judaism devoid of its element of worldliness and a Godless Paganism, there was born the Christian view, according to which a Jewish saint in the garb of a pagan man, had come to raise and prepare the nations for a better, divine world which, however, possesses all the characteristics of other-worldliness.

This other-worldliness, in the course of historical development, in the measure that the nations approached the Jewish historical religion, assumed more and more of a secular character. And the more Jewish, the more humane the pagan world became, the more

---

[31]In the Mishnah Sanhedrin, ch. V, 7, stoning and post-mortem hanging is the prescribed punishment for blasphemy and idolatry. And doubtless Jesus was executed in the same way. The Gospels, however, do not mention stoning, but speak of cruxifixion, and that as having been carried out before his death, which is certainly untrue.

[32]Graetz, *History*, Vol. III. German edition.

could Jews participate in the culture of this world and contribute to its progress. And finally, when, after the long struggle between the pagan world of sensuality and barbarous force, on the one hand, and the spiritual, mystic, Jewish view on the other, the sun of modern humanitarian civilization shed its feeble rays upon a better and more perfect world, it was a Jew who was able to signal to the world that the final stage of the process of human development has begun.

III. The Genetic View of the World

Inasmuch as Spinoza's Works have already been translated into Hebrew, the time has come when we must defend this great Jewish teacher against misrepresentation on the part of Jewish scholars. The objection raised by Luzzato against Spinoza proves only that this great Hebrew scholar has wandered into a field in which he is a total stranger. The teaching of Spinoza, which derives the entire spiritual-moral system of life from the single idea of God as the ground of Nature and Thought, and which assigns the Knowledge of God as the highest aim of life, reconciles the apparent contradiction between philosophy and experimental science on the one hand and between reason and feeling on the other. Luzzato, who charges the system of Spinoza, which is an immediate outflow of the Creative Spirit with a lack of emotion, calling it a system of dry reason, displays only his own ignorance of the true nature of these problems and of their masterly solution by Spinoza.

The basic idea of the system of Spinoza, namely, that God is the only substance, the ground and origin of all being, is the fundamental expression of the Jewish genius, which has ever manifested itself in divine revelations from the time of Moses and the Prophets, down to modern days. These manifestations of the Jewish genius are not a supernatural phenomenon, but form a part of the great eternal Law which governs all three life spheres, the cosmic, organic and social. The special field of operation of the Jewish genius, however, is the social sphere, and it is due to it that a unified historical development of humanity was made possible. The revelations of the Jewish spirit express the universal law in its entirety; its past workings as well as its future operations, using the scientific formula of to-day with the same facility as formerly the proofs of imagination and feeling.

The Jewish view, which sees in the world of Nature and life the continual operation of one creative force, is confirmed by observation. We cannot fail to conceive in any created phenomenon in Nature, or in the sphere of spirit, the immediate influence of the Creator. Those who try to avoid this conclusion, explaining the rise of beings as only a result of a mere mechanical operation of the law of cause and effect, and oppose to the theory of creation that of the eternity of matter, will find it difficult to uphold their view. The hypothesis of the eternity of the atoms of matter and of their rigidity and unchangeability does not explain all phenomena of the behavior of matter under certain conditions, and is gradually giving way to the genetic view, which sees everywhere only movements and no fixed atoms nor any stable cosmic ether, chemical atoms have not existed from eternity, but, like organic germs, were once generated and are subject to the great law of growth and decay. They arose through the act of creation, by the same act which successively calls into existence every being, and continues to form centers of gravity, which in the cosmic world we name atoms; in the organic, germs; and in the social, revelations.

Creation, however, does not mean the forming of new elements, but only a new arrangement of existing materials. Every creation is a combination of two opposite movements into a new, balanced and more perfect one. The cosmic rotation of the planetary bodies, which is the result of two opposite movements, the centripetal and the centrifugal, is an excellent illustration of this form of combination. A spiritual

93

creation is, similarly, a combination of two preceding mental tendencies into a new synthesis. Every physical creation presupposes the eternal Creator, and every spiritual creation an inspiration, which is only a channel through which the immediate influences of the Creator are conveyed. Religion is the greatest and the highest of such inspirations. Can we, then, doubt its teaching of the existence of a creative element in life, which is evidenced by experience and science; or shall we name it supernatural, an exception to the eternal law? It requires extraordinary reason to do so.

The creative process in the social life-sphere operates according to a well-formed plan, which is gradually being unfolded in history, just as a similar plan was previously developed in Nature. Spiritual creations, like the organic, have their palæontological and modern epochs, the last stage of which is the age of maturity, in which the development of social life will come to completion. The coming of the future epoch of social life will be hastened by the efforts and energy of the Jews, who have a special calling for conveying to the world revelations affecting the social life-sphere.

The typical expression of the Jewish genius, the genetic view, is essentially one with all its representatives, with Moses and the Prophets as well as with Spinoza. The first do not contradict modern science, their views are only divergent and different in external form from that of science but not contradictory to it. Nor is Spinoza's teaching contradictory to Jewish Monotheism. What Jewish revelation emphasized most is the unity of the creative spirit, in opposition to the plurality of forces; and this idea has been expressed clearly also by Spinoza. The Bible, stripped of its anthropomorphic expressions, does not offer a single point which expressly contradicts the teachings of Spinoza. Moses himself says that the Knowledge of God is not found either in heaven or in the distances of space, but that the real revelation of God takes place within ourselves, in our spirit and heart. A similar expression occurs in the Talmud. "The Holy Presence never descended to earth, nor did Moses ascend to heaven." Must we consider the anthropomorphic expressions of the Bible as dogmas? If so, they will finally undermine the fundamental dogma of Jewish teaching which is so clearly enunciated in the *Shema*. Nor is the doctrine of the eternity of the spirit to be misunderstood. The eternity of the spirit does not begin after death, but is, like God, always present.

An external God, who does not manifest himself to men as an immediate ever-present Creator, is not the God of the Jews, Christians and Mohammedans, and can become as little the religious ground of the regenerated nations as pagan Polytheism and Pantheism. A God head, of whom we know nothing, is without influence on our social, spiritual and moral life. It is only the creative God who will be the God of the age of maturity of the social life. The rationalistic view of life suits only the now antiquated form of Society, which is at present in the process of dissolution. Just as modern Nationalism is a reflection of the spirit of revolution, so is modern rationalistic supernaturalism a spiritual reflection of the reaction against the progressive social tendencies.

IV. The Last Antagonism

In order to estimate truly the spiritual attitudes toward life we must take into account the social movements of which they are the result. The present day philosophical point of view differs essentially from that held during the last century. Not only has science made tremendous progress during this time, but it has been greatly influenced by philosophical criticism and speculation, just as industry has been essentially affected by democratic revolution and the development of capitalism. The field of battle, the struggle itself and the contending forces have been changed in the historical course of the social movement, which began in the last century and which we are still continuing. The speculative philosopher of the nineteenth century has as little sympathy with the revolutionary philosopher of the eighteenth as the liberal citizen of to-day has for the revolutionist of that time. The oppressed industrial producers of the last century are the lordly speculators of our present-day Society. And even within the productive class itself, a thorough process of separation between its constituent elements has taken place. The last resolution, that which we are now witnessing, could not, therefore, have previously created a perfected organization. The old, rigid institutions of feudal Society and the last dead residue of dogmatism must first be dissected by the sharp knife of criticism and analysis, into its elements, before new social and spiritual creations can come into being. In the course of the development of new elements there came to the front a new antagonism which did not exist before, and the reconciliation of which is at present under discussion. The forces of labor in the industrial world on the one hand, and the investigators in the scientific field, on the other, liberated from the bonds of feudalism and dogmatism alike, have brought forth the last antagonism, namely, the one between labor and speculation.[33] In the revolutionary atmosphere of free competition of all labor forces, there were formed centers of gravity which will ultimately absorb the individual productive forces and organize them for their own purpose. Following the law of Gravitation, the fundamental law of all life, the single atoms of laborers grouped themselves around industrial, and the individual investigators around speculative centers. Not only in the sphere of industry but even in the field of science, it is no light task to oppose the attractive force of the speculative centers.

In merely negating the speculative system, as in merely destroying accumulated capital, we will gain but little; for all life has a natural tendency toward centralization, combination and organization. If the real producers earnestly desire to free themselves from the exploitation of the speculators, they must, following the successful attempt of English workingmen, oppose to the mass of accumulated labor in the hands of the captains of industry, on the one hand, and in the heads of the philosophic speculators on the other, the larger mass of the individual productions, as well as the results of investigations in the scientific field. This applies to scientific material as well as to industrial. Materials are only dead capital when they are not organized for further creation and production. The same law governing all productive life movements serve also for further creations out of the already gained materials. The so-called indestructibility of matter is nothing but the persistence of the productive force inherent in matter even in its dissolution and decomposition. Should the industrial and intellectual workers remain in individual isolation; should they not centralize and organize their scattered forces and become speculative in a cooperative way, the antagonism between labor and speculation will, of necessity, remain stationary.

The final theoretical antagonism which can in some measure be overcome, namely, that between philosophy and the experimental sciences, between materialism and idealism, is nothing but the theoretical expression of the practical antagonism in social life. The same attitude that the master displayed toward the slave, the priest toward the uninitiated, and later, the feudal lord toward the serf, the clerical toward the secular, is finally assumed to-day by the capitalist toward the workingman, the philosopher toward the investigator, namely, the attitude of the organized toward the unorganized and of the strong toward the weak. The people fall short in regard to the reconciliation of this antagonism. Such an attitude leads only to decomposition and death, and therefore Moses exclaimed to our people "Ye shall be unto me a kingdom of priests

[33]The words "labor" and "speculation" used by Hess here, are employed in a double sense. Labor in the industrial sense, as an economic factor, and labor as equivalent to investigation and experimentation. The first is opposed to "speculation" in its economic meaning, the second to "speculation" in its philosophic meaning, namely, theorizing.—*Translator.*

and a holy people."[34]

As industrial speculation, so philosophical speculation, is a historical necessity, and its existence is justified, as long as the productive labors and investigations are not centralized and organized, as long as they have not their own center of gravity and equilibrium. "Absolute" speculation represented, before the revolutionary critical epoch, a governing, compelling force. After this period, it is only a controlling power, strange and hostile in its attitude toward material labor. The root of this antagonism, however, lies not in the malice of this or that class, but is inherent in the history of the development of the human race which, as long as it has not reached its aim, the age of maturity, must pass toward its goal through race and class struggles, just as the human individual, while in the midst of his mental development, is dominated by one-sided representations and tendencies.

In the course of human history, only one-sided movements have arisen in social life, the influences of which have helped to engender one-sided views, representations and conceptions. During the development of organic or social life, there occurs always a division of labor among the various parts of the organisms which brings forth, along with the perfection of special functions, a certain narrowness and one-sidedness. In human life, this tendency often degenerates into a kind of monomania, the effects of which are harmful to the human spirit. But when the perfected organism of the historical races reaches its final stage of development, the various strivings of history will also reach their ultimate harmony in a perfected human society. Just as only after the completion of the organic life-sphere, namely, after the creation of man, the Sabbath of Nature began, so will the historical Sabbath begin only after the completion of the development of social life, after the creation of a harmonious social organization in which production and consumption will be in a state of equilibrium. We stand at present on the eve of the historical Sabbath. Our age is still the age of speculation. But speculation can, by its very nature, be the inheritance of only a minority. What, then, of the majority?

Every life-sphere, which has reached the completion of its development, insures the continuity of its existence, first, by means of reproduction, and, secondly, by establishing an equilibrium between production and consumption. The social life-sphere also will enter upon its age of maturity from the moment when this point of view prevails in the social economic movement. Where this point of view is only shared by a few individuals, who utilize it for private purposes, the age is dominated by speculation. The essence of speculation consists in the exploitation of the reproductive sources of social life for private purposes.

Life in general is a producing and consuming activity. Science is universal economics which investigates and determines the amount and degree of production and consumption in the various life-spheres and epochs. Physiology is the economics of the organic life-sphere, and social economy is the physiology of Society. The latter science shows us that social life is still in its childhood epoch. Between the stage of embryonic life, through which Society had passed, and the stage of maturity and independence, upon which it will enter, there lies the gap which we can hardly bridge, namely, the revolutionary critical epoch, which gave birth to modern Society, the period which made possible the independence of future social life from the past and laid the foundation of a creative Society. What revolution does for life, criticism accomplishes for ideas and views. It unfastens the chains of traditional representations which hold the present in the grip of the past, opens the way toward a new independent life, and, like revolution, considers itself independent of the creative being itself, which tradition

[34]Exodus xix, 6.

has represented as extra-mundane, as long as it has not rediscovered that creative being in the world itself. Most of our contemporaries continue to attack the external "absolute" of tradition, but they do not discover the real "Absolute," the creative center of all life, namely, the equilibrium and harmony of all spiritual forces. The few that have dared to make such a step were finally lost in speculation.

Just as the new-born babe is not entirely independent of its mother, as long as it is still being nourished by her, so social life cannot be considered emancipated until it has outgrown the nursing period. The philosophical and industrial forms of speculation employed by spiritual and material capitalists and dominating the fields of scientific and industrial labor, are the two breasts which nourish our Society, and as a result, the child—LABOR—is strongly bound to its mother—CAPITAL,—the creative spirit is chained to the former traditional achievements; and finally, the new Society is made subject to its ancient ghost. It is, therefore, the task of the intellectual, as well as the industrial workers, to liberate themselves from the domination of speculation. Scientists and Socialists should work hand in hand for the last liberation of humanity, for the emancipation of all forms of labor from speculation. And their efforts will certainly be successful, for we see that scientists in Germany and industrial laborers in England are gradually approaching the goal. But in Germany, as well as in England, these efforts are isolated; the impulse to unite both tendencies, the scientific and the industrial, can come only from the land of modern revolution and centralization—France, on the one hand, and from the Jewish people on the other, the people which has, from the beginning of its history, had for its mission, the unity of different tendencies of social life into one center of activity.

If Spinoza laid the foundation for a definite reconciliation between the two typical antithetical expressions of the human genius which reached their culminating point in the creations of the Greeks and the Jews, then it became the task of history after Spinoza to develop the seed which he had sown, into a definite reconciliation of all antagonism in the life of nations.

German philosophy undoubtedly rendered a great service when it succeeded in overcoming, on the basis laid by Spinoza's conception of Jewish monotheism, the opposition of atheism to theism, which was expressed so clearly by the revolutionary thinkers. But at the same time, this philosophy lacked a positive foundation in life and experimental science, and as a result, it must have necessarily come into conflict with the latter. The last form of antagonism, which is still to be reconciled, is not the one between Monotheism and Polytheism, as in antiquity, nor between Moslem Monism and Christian Dualism, as in the Mediæval Ages, nor between Theism and Atheism, but between speculative philosophy and experimental science. The German scientists are called to the mission of reconciling this last form of antagonism by work like Moleschott's, which will ultimately lead to the merging of science into philosophy and philosophy into science. It is in Germany, where experimental science will be emancipated by means of a cooperative activity on the part of the scientists, to gather all data collected in different fields and interpret them from a general point of view, so as to bring all the various parts into a harmonious, organic whole.

V. THE LAST RACE RULE

The more perfect a people is in its own special calling, the more it appreciates the particular services of other peoples, and the more willingly it borrows from them the ideas, conceptions and inventions which are necessary to modern life. This tendency is especially noticeable in the German people and it certainly does honor to the German spirit.

The Jewish nation, therefore, must not hesitate to follow France in all matters relating to the political and social regeneration of the nations, and especially in what concerns its own rebirth as a nation, on the one hand; and in everything which bears upon the revival of intellectual life in Germany on the other. Only a stupid reaction, which is consciously or unconsciously swept along by its own alarm, can bear us malice when we sympathize with France in all matters of a social, political nature, and yet try to absorb and assimilate everything good in German spiritual and intellectual life.

The cause of national regeneration of oppressed peoples can expect no help and sympathy from Germany. The problem of regeneration, which dates not from the second restoration of the kingdom in France, but goes back to the French Revolution, the definite solution of which began in Europe only recently, with the outbreak of the Italian war, was received in Germany with mockery and derision; and in spite of the fact that the question is an urgent one and is uppermost almost everywhere, even in Germany itself, the Germans have named it the "Nationality trick." Our Jewish democrats, also, display their patriotism in accusing the French and the peoples sympathizing with them, of conquering designs. The French, say the German politicians, as well as the allies, will only be exploited by the second Monarchy, for purposes of restraining liberty rather than promoting it. It is, therefore, according to the deep logic of these politicians, the duty of the German to be obedient to the Kaiser and the kings, in order that they should be able to defeat the conquering desires of the French. These politicians and patriots forget, that if Germany were to conquer France and Italy to-day, it would only result in placing the entire German people under police law; and in depriving the Jews of their civil rights, in a worse manner than after the Way of Liberation, when the only reward granted by the Germans to their Jewish brethren in arms was exclusion from civil life. And, truly, the German people and the German Jews do not deserve any better lot when they allow themselves, in spite of the examples of history, to be entrapped by Mediæval reaction.

Scientific studies, together with my life experiences, have matured my political sympathies for France, especially after I learned to know the people. I have formulated my thoughts in the following sentences:

Social life-tendencies are, like spiritual life-views, typical and primal race creations. The entire past history of humanity originally moved only in the circle of race and class struggle. The race struggle is the primal one, and the class struggle secondary. The last dominating race is the German. But, thanks to the French people, which succeeded not only in reconciling race antagonism in its own land, but also uprooted every form of race domination within the borders of France, the race struggle is nearing its end. And along with the cessation of race antagonism, the class struggle will also come to a standstill. The equalization of all classes of Society will necessarily follow the emancipation of the races, for it will ultimately become only a scientific question of social economics.

Yet it seems that a final race struggle is unavoidable, if the German politicians, failing to grasp the situation, do not attempt to oppose the tremendous current of reaction, which will ultimately involve Germany in a collision with the Romance nations, and will also entrap the progressive German democrats in the net of Romantic demagogy. Mediæval reaction succeeded twice during the present century, once during the "War of Liberation," and for the second time, during the Italian war, in defeating the modern efforts of the German people for political and social regeneration, by inflaming the race dominance instincts in the hearts of the lords of war, who think themselves lords of the land by divine right, and consider the people as their rightly inherited slaves. It is not impossible, that in case of a war between Italy and Austria,

German democracy will, for the third time, be engulfed by the whirl of reaction and join her in a war for race dominance, the results of which will be detrimental to progress. But out of the last race struggle, which Ferdinand Freiligrath has vividly depicted in his vision "At the Birch Tree;" there will arise no new domination of any race, and the equality of all world historical peoples will follow as a necessary result.

VI. A Chapter of History

Nations like individuals pass, in the course of their development, through certain definite life-periods. Not every age is adapted for every stage of development; but every age has its particular degree of progress. And if a people is belated in its development or has missed one of the stages, it will be very difficult for it to follow the harmonious march of nations toward progress.

Germany at the time of the Reformation, occupied a high position in the field of social and political development. Even the masses were permeated with the spirit of social-political reform, the like of which was seen only in England in the seventeenth century and in France in the eighteenth. The sixteenth century was the epoch of the German Renaissance. Germany, during that period, gave birth to a great reform, but inasmuch as it did not succeed in becoming a truly national reform, it only divided the nation into two. The political-social revolution of the peasants, on the other hand was finally drowned in their own blood.

Had not the uprising of the peasants been shamefully betrayed by the leaders of German culture and civilization, the development of the nation would, at that time, have already assumed a normal form, and not only would Germany be the equal of the other civilized nations, but as the first-born modern nation, would have held the roost prominent place among them. The might of the Mediæval "German Sword" would have been transformed into the nobler and higher force of the modern German spirit. The nation which overthrew the world empire of Rome, in order to substitute for it the Mediæval feudal power, would have been the first to give the signal for the overthrow of its own institutions, the overthrow of the last form of race dominance. But Fate willed otherwise. The last chosen people, like the first, must atone for its sins before it is granted the privilege of leading its historical rôle, before it will be worthy to enter into the modern alliance of humanity, which is based on the equality of all historical nations.

The external causes which brought about the nipping in the bud of the German revolution are well known. Charles the Fifth, who, at the time of the awakening of a national consciousness among the historical nations, strove to realize his dream of a world German-Roman empire, was one of the chief factors in causing the destruction of the popular revolution. This monarch missed his great opportunity to raise Germany, by means of supporting social, political and religious reform, to the dignity of a useful modern State, to liberate it from the yoke of Feudalism and save it from disruption, and finally to create for himself a nation and to give to the people a real king, to create a modern monarchy which would support all the oppressed peoples and terrify the conquering Mediæval lords of war. But, through his wavering conduct, the contrary result occurred. The nobility could free themselves from the subjection to the Emperor, on the one hand, by joining with the new religious reform, and from the influence of the people, on the other, by suppressing the political social uprising; and consequently they followed this course of action. This anti-national activity was furthered, not only by the contradictory policy of the German Emperor and the ambition of the nobles, but also by the political inability of the leader of the Reformation. Luther, with his doctrinal stupidity, thought it more advantageous to join the nobility rather than the common people and finally betrayed the peasants, just as, even to-day, the German doctrinaires are always ready to betray the people whenever they attempt to take the democratic movement seriously. And yet, in spite of all these difficulties, the German revolution would have triumphed, had it not been for the fact that the cities, the seat of a social class, which had immediate interest in the downfall of Feudalism, were too narrow-minded and cowardly at heart to see the great importance of the peasant uprising and to struggle for their own liberation. Having been delivered into the hands of their enemies by their natural allies, denounced in shameful orations by the German reformer, forsaken by the Emperor and butchered by the hereditary warlords, the German peasants were forced to abandon the revolution, along with which was also nipped in the bud the germ of Germany's regeneration. And from that moment, the German nations began to descend lower and lower in the scale of progress. Luther, who lacked no insight into human affairs, saw it and expressed himself sorrowfully about it.

The punishment for this great crime against the people on the part of the nobles and citizens came but too soon. In the Thirty Years War, the German cities had to submit involuntarily to the sentence which they themselves, by their breaking away from the German revolution, had thus pronounced. They could then see that "the history of the world is the world's Court of Justice," but they could not avert the fated doom. For at the time when the English revolution raised our proud neighbor to the height of culture and civilization and laid the foundation of its present world power, Germany was bleeding white through its civil and religious wars, and this process was repeated many times. Even the French Revolution, which taught all European nations to love and esteem liberty, brought to Germany only the shame of foreign rule and the still worse domination of the reaction, which since then settled so securely upon the back of the German people, that not even the revolutions of 1830 and 1848 could, in any way, overthrow it from its seat. And just as at the time of the first French Revolution, German literature and philosophy, which were then at their height, could not protect the ghost of a German empire from its fate, so are all our orators, writers and poets of to-day unable to revive the political corpse of Germany, the soul of which had departed long ago in the unfortunate peasant war. Great popular leaders and patriotic heroes do not descend from the skies, but grow out of the deep soil of the people and its history. When the latter is arrested in the midst of its flight toward progress, the political genius of the nation must necessarily be extinguished.

And this is just what happened in Germany. At the time of the peasant war, Germany possessed great statesmen, who united in their persons patriotism and modernity and were also able to train the people and implant in them the same traits. To-day these people lack the common soil and traditions necessary for development of statesmen of such stamp. All reminiscences of German greatness go back either to Mediæval times or further back to the primitive forests. The present German patriotism is reactionary and has no root in the life of the people. As long as it is impossible to realize the aim of a modern German movement, so long can there exist no modern German people.

Without regeneration there can be no people, and without a people, in the modern sense of the word, there can be no modern patriotism. Present-day German patriotism, which expresses itself only in verbal protestations against our neighbors, while it has neither the courage nor the talent to occupy itself with the work of regeneration, is only an air bubble. Germany does not suffer from the oppression of a foreign yoke, nor is there any fear that it will suffer in the future, as the patriots would have us believe, but it is ailing as a result of its murdered revolution; it can no more make the same move toward progress without the help of the other progressive European nations. The Germans are too proud to join forces with those nations which succeeded in liberating themselves from the Christian Mediæval spirit. Hence they will have to be subjected to a Mediæval reaction, which they did not know how to defeat at the right moment.

The last opportunity, which offered us the elevation of the German people to the degree of a modern nation, namely, the "War of Liberation,"[35] ended only in a victory for reaction; for the war against France was a war of reactionary Europe against the spirit of the French Revolution. And were Germany to go to war again with any nation, the same result would be repeated; a victory of the army would be a victory of reaction. So deeply have we sunk, that we are forced to hail a defeat of the army as a happy event in the history of the German people. Indeed, "the history of the world is the world's Court of Justice." We must atone now for the sins we committed in the sixteenth century.

Who can foresee the catastrophes that may befall us as a result of our arrested development? Certainly, we hope that the struggle of the German people will come to an end with the equalization of all oppressed peoples which struggle to attain the same aim. But by what means the goal will be reached, no one knows. What peaceful or warlike German patriot dares to think about it?

The age of race dominance is at an end. Even the smallest people, whether it belongs to the Germanic or Romance, Slavic or Finnic, Celtic or Semitic races, as soon as it advances its claims to a place among the historical nations, will find sympathetic supporters in the powerful civilized Western nations. Like the patriots of other unfortunate nations, the German patriots can attain their aim only by means of a friendly alliance with the progressive and powerful nations of the world. But if they continue to conjure themselves, as well as the German people, with the might and glory of the "German Sword," they will only add to the old unpardonable mistakes, grave new ones; they will only play into the hands of the reaction, and drag all Germany along with them.

[35]"The War of Liberation," referred to by Hess, is the war of the year 1813-14, which Germany, in conjunction with her allies, Russia and Great Britain, waged against Napoleon.—*Translator.*

NOTES

NOTE I

The Talmud as well as the Midrash, ascribe the redemption of Israel from Egypt to the chastity of the Jewish women and their faithfulness to the Jewish nationality. It is especially emphasized that the Jews in Egypt retained their national names and language and did not adopt the names and language of the Egyptians and were thus more worthy of redemption than the exiles of later generations, when this form of assimilation was a frequent phenomenon. Witness the following passages:[1]

"Our ancestors did not change their names in Egypt. Those who went down to Egypt went by the names of Reuben and Simeon, and their descendants, who left Egypt, have continued to bear the same names. Judah was not changed to Rufus, nor Reuben to Lulianus nor Joseph to Lustus nor Benjamin to Alexander."

Even our greatest prophet and lawgiver, Moses, is severely blamed for his posing before the daughters of Jethro as an Egyptian, and not as a Hebrew. And because of that, the Midrash asserts, God refused his plea to be buried in the Holy Land; while Joseph, who never denied his descent, was rewarded by being carried to the Holy Land and buried there.

Said Moses to God: "Lord of the world, the bones of Joseph were interred in the Holy Land; why dost thou not grant me the same privilege?" Said the Holy One, blessed be He: "The one who acknowledged his land deserved to rest there, but the one who denied it will not be interred in her sacred soil. Whence do we know that Joseph acknowledged his land? We know it from the following: When his mistress complained of Joseph to her husband in the words 'Behold he has brought here a Hebrew to mock at us,' Joseph did not deny that he was a Hebrew but affirmed it and, when brought before Pharaoh, he proudly exclaimed: 'I was stolen from the land of the Hebrews.' He was therefore buried in his own land. But thou, who didst deny thy land, wilt not be buried in thy land; for when the daughters of Jethro said, "An Egyptian saved us from the hands of the shepherds," thou didst hear it and wast silent and therefore thou wilt not be buried in thy land.[2]

NOTE II

The extra-mundane point of support which the Jewish historical religion has in common with the Natural Religion of the Hindus, is the point of contact between the Jewish and the Pagan, the Semitic and the Indo-Germanic world views, the germ out of which the Mediæval Christian and the modern scientific views of life have grown. Here, in this *punctum saliens,* there meet the two great mental expressions of the two great historical races. Both recognized and expressed clearly in their oldest literary documents, that the ordinary relations of life become cumbersome to man as soon as his spirit awakens in him, and that holiness then becomes a necessary condition of salvation. Both dreamed of a golden age in the distant past, of a Paradise lost which, however, they hope that man will once more regain. But in human life there goes on a continuous struggle between the elementary demands and the human tendencies which contain the germ of the harmonious unity of life, the goal of the history of humanity. To help the human spirit in its struggle, both religions preach restraint from the pleasures of life, which bring only death and misery in their wake, as a means to attain holiness and salvation. But there is a difference in their preaching, and this difference expresses the essential separation of the two world views. The ascetic

[1]Midrash Rabba, Numbers, Ch. 20, also Canticles, Ch. 4, Leviticus, Ch. 32.
[2]Midrash Rabba Deuteronomy, Ch. 2.

tendency of the Indo-Germanic race, the contemplative character of which has never spurred it on to an active life, finally expressed itself in a complete renunciation and negation of life (viz.: Brahmanism and Buddhism). The Jews, on the other hand, from the beginning of their history and throughout the storms of their exile, have clung fast to their mission, namely, to bring about the sanctification, not only of individual life, but also of the social life of Man, to further its development and to prepare humanity for the Messianic time which will be an age of perfected development and holiness.

The spirit of Hindu wisdom found its best and purest expression in the writing of a pure-blooded German, Schopenhauer, whose works ought to form a part of the mental equipment of every educated man. Schopenhauer represents, within the Christian-German world, the most decided contrasting tendency to the teachings of Hegel. The latter allowed the historical, the genetic view of the world, the Jewish view, to be the generating point of the spirit and thus raised the concrete Jewish historical religion to the heights of an abstract spiritual philosophy. Schopenhauer, on the other hand, negates historical religion completely, and along with it, historical development, nay, even life itself in all its forms, ideal as well as real. This destructive nihilism, which is an original trait of the Indo-Germanic race, and from the beginning found its clearest expression in India, gradually undermined the entire structure of Natural Religion and finally brought about its complete dissolution. Only the genetic view of life, that the Judaism, which incorporated a partial negation of the natural world, without at the same time minimizing the value of the creative human factor in history, was able to enrich the world with a more confident and self-reliant conception which pieced together the fragments of a tottering world and united them once more into an integral world by means of the hope for a future regeneration.

If we agree with Schopenhauer that the creative being is only an elementary natural force and not the creative genius of all historical development in Nature as well as in History, we must also accept the world as product of self-contradictory and self-destructive forces, the striving of which, expressed in Schopenhauer's formula, "The will to live", is without aim and purpose, and offers no satisfaction to the moral and intellectual man. Only historical religion, which see in the struggle of natural forces, as in that of individuals and nations, only stages of development, and which carries within itself the confidence of the final victory of the Divine Power, needs not negate life in order to reach its sanctification. And even the very sanctity of life, which Hinduism preaches, is, in its content, only a contemplative egoism which is of little use to humanity. Every striving toward a better state of existence, whether it be an ideal or a real one, in this world or in the next, appears to this contemplative egoism as pure silliness. Striving is conceived by it as an attempt to perpetuate the raw elementary struggle, the *bellum omnium contra omnes,* the war of all against all. This anti-genetic view manifest itself in all social movements as a conservative or reactionary force. Schopenhauer himself, as is known, turned over his capital to a Berlin Society, the purpose of which was to carry on a campaign against the champions of the people. His endorsement of Christianity applies only to its negative phase, in which lies its essential difference from Judaism, namely, its disparagement of the present life, but does not include its positive side, the exaltation of regeneration, by means of which Christianity converted the pagan world to Jewish religious point of view and thus reconciled it with life.

We do not, however, want to deny the fact that contrary results have often occurred. The holders of the contemplative view, who have sometimes gone so far as to negate the very will to live, have at times been able to create great artistic works and also to enjoy them, while those who have followed the "Kingdom of Heaven" namely the mission to organize social life on the divine plan, have by no means had their way strewn with roses.

Note III

In 1858, there appeared, at Leipzig, a work written by Otto Wigand under the title *Two discourses concerning the desertion from Judaism*, being an analysis of the views on this question expressed in the recently published correspondence of Dr. Abraham Geiger. The author endeavors to prove that the conclusions of Dr. Geiger are untenable both from a philosophic and from a social standpoint. Here are his social arguments:

"My friend," says the author, "there are certain conclusions which you cannot escape. The stamp of slavery, if we may use this expression, which centuries of oppression have deeply impressed upon the Jewish features, might have been obliterated by the blessed hand of regained civil liberty. The gait of the Jews, buoyed up by the happy reminiscences of the victory won in the struggle for the noble possession of liberty, might have been straighter and prouder. The Jewish face may certainly beam with pride, as it views the tremendous progress made by the Jews in a brief time, their mighty flight to the spiritual height upon which they now stand, which is especially notable considering the fact that their poets and writers at whose greatness the nation is astonished, and of whose talents the entire people takes account, have sprung from those who, a generation again, could hardly converse correctly in the language of the land. Such a state of affairs should undoubtedly call forth admiration in the hearts of the present German generation, and yet, in spite of the achievements, the wall separating the Jew and the Christian still stands unshattered, for the watchman that guards them is one who will not be caught napping. It is the race difference between the Jewish and Christian populations. If this assertion of mine surprises or astonishes you, I ask you to consider whether it is not almost a rule with the Germans that race differences generate prejudices which cannot be overcome by any manifestation of good-will on the part of the other race. The relations existing between the German and the Slavic populations in Bohemia, in Hungary and Transylvania, between the Germans and the Danes in Schleswig, or between the Irish and the Anglo-Saxon settlers in Ireland, illustrates well the power of race antagonism in the German world. In all these countries the different elements of the population have lived side by side for centuries, sharing equally all political rights, and yet, so strong are the national or racial differences, that a social amalgamation of the various elements of the population is even at the present day quite unthinkable. And what comparison is there between the race differences of a German and Slav, a Celt and Anglo-Saxon, or a German and Dane, and the race antagonism between the children of the sons of Jacob, who are of Asiatic descent, and the descendants of Teut and Herman, the ancestors of whom have inhabited Europe from time immemorial; between the proud and the tall blond German and the small of figure, black-haired and black-eyed? Races which differ in such a degree oppose each other instinctively and against such opposition reason and good sense are powerless."

These expressions are certainly frank and sincere in their meaning, though they by no means prove the conclusions to which the author wishes to arrive, namely, the desirability of conversion; for conversion will not turn a Jew into a German. But they at least contain the confession, that an instinctive race antagonism triumphs in Germany above all humanitarian sentiments. The "pure human nature" resolves itself, according to the Germans, in the nature of pure Germanism. The "high-born blond" looks with contempt upon the regeneration of the "black-haired, quick-moving mannikins," without regard to whether they are descendants of the Biblical patriarchs, or of the ancient Romans and Gauls.

While other civilized western nations mention the shameful oppression to which the Jews were formerly subjected, only as an act of theirs of which they are ashamed, the German remembers only the "stamp of slavery" which he impressed upon "the Jewish physiognomy."

In a *feuilleton* which appeared recently in the *Bonnerzeitung,* entitled "Bonn Eighty Years Ago," the author speaks of the Jews in mocking terms and describes them as people who lived in separate quarters and supported themselves by petty trades. I believe that we should wonder less at the fact that the Jews, who were forbidden to participate in the important branches of industry and commerce, lived on petty trade, than at the fact they were able to live at all in those centuries of oppression. As a matter of fact, almost every means of existence, including the right of domicile, was denied them. It was only by means of bribes that every Jewish generation could procure anew the "privilege" not to be driven out of their homes in Bonn, and they felt happy indeed if, in spite of the contract, they were not robbed of their property and exiled, or attacked by a fanatical mob in the bargain. I, also, can tell a story of "eighty years ago." A Jew won the high favor of the Kurfuerst of Bonn, that he and his descendants were granted the "privilege" to settle in Ebendich.[3]

Note IV

Gabriel Riesser, the editor of the magazine, *The Jew,* as far as I can recollect, never fell into the error, common to all modern German Jews, that the emancipation of the Jews is irreconcilable with the development of Jewish Nationalism. He demanded emancipation for the Jews on the one condition only, that of their receiving all civil and political rights in return for their assuming all civil and political burdens.

Suppose we assume that the Jews had not only a national religion, but a real nationality, a land and a State, and that, as happens with all other nations, a number of this sovereign State were to settle in foreign countries, and to live their for centuries, would those countries deny them the right of naturalization if they, in return for civil and political rights undertook to discharge all duties and bear all the burdens of the State? Is it not sufficient for a person to be born in a country, or even to prove that he has lived in country for a number of years, to be entitled to citizenship after the expiration of a certain time? In countries which stand at present at the height of civilization, this is an accepted fact, but not in Germany. Here, the Jews, who has lived in the land for centuries, must first deny his race, his descent, his traditional memories, his type and temperament, nay, even his very character, in order to prove himself worthy to live among a people which will not contribute anything to modern civil and political life, unless it overcomes its inherited race prejudices. The Jews, on the other hand, have never been dominated by prejudice nor actuated by the desire of race mastery. The fundamental law of the Mosaic polity enunciates explicitly the equality of all inhabitants of the land of Israel, without regard as to whether they are Jews or foreigners.

Note V

At the time of Mendelssohn's activity in Germany, there lived in Poland a man by the name Israel Bal Shem. He, like Mendelssohn had dreamed very little that he would some day become the founder of a sect. And yet, just as in spite of his personal wishes, Mendelssohn was proclaimed the originator of the Reform movement, so it was through Israel Bal Shem that the Chasidic sect of the Slavic countries was called into life. The word *chasid,* in its literal meaning, is the appellation given to every pious Jew and connotes, unlike the word "pietist" in Protestant Christianity, no secondary

---

[3]Ebendich is a village near Bonn.

meaning. There have been Chasidim among the Jews at all times, just as there were long before the so-called Bal Shem, Jews who devoted themselves to the mystic teachings of the Kabbala and who were said to perform miracles by means of practical Kabbala. But there were also, on the other hand, in former generations, Jews who participated in the culture of the land where they dwelt, in the same measure as the Jews of Germany since Mendelssohn have participated in German culture, and yet they, unlike the latter, did not call themselves reformers. Therefore, if Rationalism among the German Jews, on the one hand, and Chasidim among the Slavonian Jews on the other, did call forth a grave schism among the Jews of those countries, the causes for it lie not in the nature of the tendencies themselves but in the peculiar condition of the ages of their birth. Especially is this true of Slavonic lands, where the spirit of the times had not penetrated the consciousness of the masses.

The Chasidim, like the Jewish Essenes in the last period of antiquity, and like the Christian pietists at the end of the Middle Ages, represent a tendency which emphasizes more the inner essence of religion than the mere external performance of its precepts. The Chasidim do not observe pedantically all the minutiae of Jewish law, though they do not deny nor question in the least, the authority of both the written and the oral law; but they believe that both the written and the oral law are an expression of the spirit, and that in this consists their real value. Not the form, but the spirit which created it, is for them the holy and the sacred. And yet they are not less ascetical than other pious Jews but observe strictly all the laws of morality and purity. Their answer to the rabbis who accuse them of transgressing certain laws and precepts is "We are not subjected to the *Midath hadin,* i.e., God's strict measure of judgment, but to the *Midath harachamim,* i.e., His measure of grace and mercy. The philosophical aspect of Chasidim, from the point of view of theoretical Kabbala, is developed by Rabbi Samuel of Wilna in his book, the *Tanya.* The disciples of this philosopher call themselves *Chabad* (a word that is formed from the initials of three Hebrew words *Chokmah*—wisdom, *Bina*—treason, and *Daath*—knowledge. This sect is widely scattered among the Jews and is even represented in Jerusalem.

As regards the form which Chasidism assumed among the Jewish masses of Poland and other Slavonic countries, as well as in Hungary, it is undoubtedly not free from gross superstitions; yet the critics, who rightly combat this degenerating tendency of Chasidism do not, after all, seem to conceive the proper essence nor the historical importance of Chasidism. The rabbis, as well as the Rationalists, have attempted to declare Chasidism a heresy; but their arrows of excommunication had as little effect as the criticism of the Rationalists, against a spiritual tendency which was, like Reform, the product of the age, and, though of an unconscious nature, and perhaps because of that of great importance. The Reform movement in Germany rose only after modern life had completely undermined Mediæval Judaism and closed up its life source. It could, therefore, only utilize the remnants of a Judaism torn away from its main trunk, as timber or ornaments for its essentially non-Jewish temple. Chasidism, on the other hand, built its house and developed within the folds of the living spirit of a Judaism which was influenced, more instinctively than consciously, by the spirit of modern times, and thus formed a transition from Mediæval Judaism to a regenerated Judaism, which is still to be conceived as being in the process of development. The great good which will result from a combination of Chasidism with the national movement is almost incalculable. Chasidism makes great gains in the great Jewish centers of the East. Even the rabbis, who heretofore have declared Chasidism a heresy, are beginning to understand that there are only two alternatives for the great Jewish masses of Eastern Europe; either to be absorbed along with the reformers, by the gradually penetrating external culture, or to avert this catastrophe by an inner regeneration of which Chasidism is certainly a forerunner.

Although the Chasidim are without social organization, they live in socialistic fashion. The house of the rich man is always open to the poor and the latter is as much at home there as he is in his own house. They seem to have taken as their motto the saying in Aboth: "He who says what is mine is thine and what is thine is thine is a saint"[4] (Aboth, v:13). A sect which practises such self-abnegation and whose members are capable of great religious enthusiasm must have for its foundation something more than mere crudeness and ignorance.[5]

NOTE VI

The Greeks had sanctified and worshiped Nature in their religious cult only in its finished and harmonious form, but not in its creative and becoming aspect. Man, also, had been deified in the Grecian world only as a complete organization, as a being who stands at the height of organic life, but not as the representative of a new life sphere; not as a moral and social being, who is to be looked upon as in the midst of becoming and developing, as is the case with Christianity, the descendant of the historical religion of Judaism. The Jews, on the other hand, had turned the tables, deifying *the becoming;* worshiping the God whose very name expresses past, present and future. Even the cosmic and organic life spheres, which are already completed in this universal epoch, are not considered by the Bible as eternal and unchangeable, but viewed from the creative standpoint. The Bible begins with the creation of the world and the declaration of the natural Sabbath, but the prophets have gone further and completed the process, embracing as they did the entire history of human development and foreseeing the final historical Sabbath. The tendency to view God in history, not only in the history of humanity, but also in the history of the cosmic and organic world, is an essential expression of the Jewish spirit. This striving after the recognition of God is developed in historical studies, through observation of historical facts; but in nature-study, it posits a certain mental direction as a starting-point, one that is totally unknown to modern scientists. Goethe and Humboldt were utterly opposed to the tendency of spiritualizing Nature, which is so closely united with the Jewish God-idea.

The Greeks sanctified the totality of Nature, including man as a complete product; the Jews sanctified the totality of history, including that of the organic and cosmic life; and the Christian deified and sanctified the individual. Individuality had thus found its complete expression through Christian apotheosis. Such a view does man both justice and injustice; for in order to delineate the rights of the individual, man must be conceived abstractly and not as he really exists, united with Nature and history, family

[4]According to the Mishnah in Aboth, there are four points of view as regards "Mine" and "Thine." The first has already been discussed by us in the third letter. It is the ordinary bourgeois rule of conduct, namely, "Everyone for himself." The second is that of the boor—the *Am Haaretz.* Who would share the riches of the wealthy and give him in exchange his own meager share, changing places with him, so to speak. The third is the view of the *Chasid* who says, "mine is thine," without desiring anything in return. The fourth is the attitude of the wicked who desires the property of others without giving anything in return.

[5]Hess's estimate of the Chasidim and Chasidism is exaggerated. Chasidism does not represent a great spiritual revolution in the history of Judiasm, as some assert, nor was it a fore-runner of the greater inner regeneration, as Hess would have us believe. Its latest development certainly does not entitle it to that exalted position. Only one or two of its leader have risen to a philosophic conception of Judaism. Equally exaggerated is the attribution to the Chasidim of an anti-legal tendency and the supplying of it with philosophic reasons. On the contrary, the great majority of the Chasidim are more careful observers of all the minutiae of the law than their opponents. It is true that law-breakers were found among the leaders of the Chasidim, especially in the early days of the sect, but their reason for law-breaking was of more material nature than the philosophic distinction between kernel and husk, though they certainly endeavored to reduce their transgressions to a religious system. But to take them seriously and to charge their actions to the account of Chasidism, is pure exaggeration. Hess however knew very little about the Chasidim and derived his information from books, and was thus often grossly misinformed. He attributes the founding of the *Chabad* to one, Samuel of Wilna, a totally unknown personality, when it is well known that the founder was Shneor Zalman of Ladie who was also the author of the *Tanya.* Wilna, on the other hand, was the fortress of opposition to Chasidism.—*Translator.*

and country. The fall of the ancient world and the entry of the Germanic race upon the arena of history have brought about both the strengthening of individuality and its one-sidedness, which to-day is undermining individuality, but true personality will rise again when individualism will be united with other higher tendencies. The realization of this higher unity can be made possible only by viewing the Jewish historical religion in a scientific manner. The religion which will be raised to a science is none other than the Bible religion, which preaches the genesis and the unity of cosmic, organic and social life, and to the development and spread of which, the genius of the Jews after their regeneration as an independent nation, will be devoted.

Note VII

At the boundary line of time, which led from the natural, organic life of the prehistoric races to the social life of the historical nations, the first, according to the story of the Book of Genesis, were doomed to destruction with the rather unintelligible words, "My spirit will not dwell forever in man because he is flesh." Everything which is generated must eventually disappear. Nothing in existence persists eternally, neither an atom nor an entire planet, neither the germ out of which whole generations had developed, nor the highest being of the earth, man, "because he is flesh" and must therefore follow the way of all fleshy namely, death and dissolution.

All nations of antiquity had their legends about the final catastrophe of all organic life. But it was left to our Jewish genetic view, which had penetrated deeply into the very essence of the created world, to conceive "being" as "becoming," a conception which reconciles the antithesis of life and death, and sees reality as an everlasting succession of birth and rebirth.

The anti genetic, pagan view of the world, which taught the eternity of being, has avoided, whenever possible, the question of becoming. But modern science has forced this old view to withdraw from its position. The phenomenon of the rise and decay of individual entities—and all temporal-spatial existence is individual, namely, limited—looms so largely in the whole organic life-sphere, that the pagan view of the eternity of being long ago recognized its dangerous position and sought refuge in the theory of the pre-existence of the germs or atoms.

[*Note*—What follows is too abstruse to reproduce in its entirety. We will therefore only give the gist of Hess's arguments, omitting the scientific proofs.]

Hess attempts to disprove first the theory of the preexistence of the germ, by asserting that the germ itself is being regenerated through the process of metabolism and so is the body constantly rebuilt after its full development and full growth by the process of continual cell formation. The germ, therefore, is not a fixed preexisting thing, but only a stage in the flowing process of life. This process runs in a cycle, embracing also the phenomenon which is apparently the opposite of life, namely, death. But in reality, death is only a step in the great process of life; for every new formation of life is preceded by the dissolution of its preceding form.

Moreover, not only are germs fixed and themselves generated from organic matter, but they are even sometimes formed from inorganic matter. And this was certainly the case at the beginning of the development of the life-sphere. Cases of spontaneous generation, i.e., cases where life springs up anew without a preceding life, occur often. He quotes a number of experiments and testimonies of travelers to corroborate his view. Hess, as a philosophic creationist, who sees in life as well as in other spheres of the universe new combinations, cannot adopt the Darwinian view which applies rather a mechanical explanation to the origin of species. He combats this view and believes that the species are constant and do not pass into one another by mutation, but new species arise in a spontaneous manner through the mediation of existing species.

The third point which Hess endeavors to establish is the perishability of atoms. He attempts to disprove the doctrine of the eternity of atoms and maintains that cosmic matter, in the form of cosmic atoms, came into being out of rarified space by a creative act. For proofs of his cosmic theory he refers to his articles on the subject in the scientific magazines. *Century* and *Natur,* Thus Hess endeavors to establish his genetic philosophy by a peculiar scientific system. He lays special emphasis on the law of conservation of energy and sees in it a corroboration of the Jewish idea of the oneness and uniqueness of the creative being. He applies this law to the social world. An exact Social Science does not as yet exist. Science has hitherto had for its object only Nature, namely, the cosmic and organic life-spheres. The reason for it is that the possible object of a Social Science, namely, the social world, is still in the process of becoming, but science deals with objective and concrete things. And this is the reason that science has little to do with religion; for religion, as well as morality, is a product of social life. The adoption of the Jewish idea of the unity of life by science will be accomplished in the following manner: Science will, on the one hand, abandon the pagan conception of the eternity of matter or atoms, and, on the other hand, will purge the idea of unity from its anthropomorphic elements with which the racial genius had endowed it, and which prevented it from deeply influencing the social, human life. It is only after the complete development of the human and social life that science will perform its proper function and vindicate its utility.

Note VIII

Luzzato expresses himself quite frankly concerning the sacrificial cult; he assigns to it a pre-Mosaic origin. The word *Kadosh*—holy, which is undoubtedly older than the Mosaic law, is derived, according to him, from the words *Yekod esh*—burned by fire, referring to the ancient usage of burning all sacrifices. Luzzato speaks with authority. According to him, the sacrificial cult described in the Bible was a concession made by Moses to the popular beliefs of the children of Israel, in order to forestall a reversion to paganism. It had also another purpose, namely, to strengthen the unity of the people, by compelling them to bring their sacrifices to one place, the Temple at Jerusalem. It had likewise a charitable aim in view when it prescribed that every voluntary offering must be immediately consumed, for thus it often happened that the poor were invited to the sacrificial feast. Just as with the paschal lamb, so it was with many free-will offerings; almost every head of a family brought an offering at least once a year; and thus the sacrificial cult really formed the basis of Jewish solidarity which is so practically expressed in the saying: "All Jews are responsible for one another."

Maimonides goes still further, and sees in the limitation of the sacrificial cult to one place a tendency to restrain its practise. He, like other thinkers, considers the sacrificial cult a concession to pagan forms of worship, but he emphasizes the fact that the purpose of Moses was to displace, by means of the sacrificial ceremonies, the practise of human sacrifices, which was widespread among the nations of the East. A similar explanation is offered by Abarbanel in his commentary to Exodus, namely, that the sacrifice of the paschal lamb was instituted to divert the people from the worship of the Egyptian god Ammon, who was represented as having a lamb's head.

It is certain that the practise of human sacrifices, which was common to all nations of antiquity, was displaced only after great effort, by the gradual spread of the institution of animal sacrifices. The history of antiquity, Biblical as well as pagan, proves this assertion. The story of the trial of Abraham, where the angel, immediately after refusing to accept the sacrifice of Isaac, substitutes the animal in his place, reflects this tendency. A similar meaning is to be seen in the story of Euripides, where Artemis had taken Iphigenia from the sacrificial stall, a deer was found in her place. But custom dies hard, and long after it ceases to exist, traces of it still survive. Such traces of human sacrifice we find both in the Old Testament[6] and in Grecian legend. Iphigenia herself, after she escapes from Aulis, reappears on Mount Tauris as a Priestess of Artemis and is by her commanded to sacrifice every Greek appearing on the mountain. More widely spread and more deeply rooted in the life of the people than among the pre-biblical kinsmen of the Jews and the Greeks, were human sacrifices among the other nations of antiquity. In India, in Egypt, in ancient Germany, as well as among the Semitic nations, human sacrifices had been widely practised. The Franks, who accompanied King Theudobert on his march into Italy, sacrificed the women and children of captive Goths, throwing the first-fruits of their victory into the Po.[7] The view that a human sacrifice was required in order to propitiate the wrath of God, persisted even in the Christian world, which looks upon the Crucifixion of Jesus as a sacrifice of atonement. Echoes of this conception, though not as gross, we find also in the Zohar, where it is said: "The innocent sometimes serves as an offering to atone for the sins of others, and therefore do the pious suffer to atone for the sins of the world."[8] The slaughter of a rooster for each male member of the family and of a hen for each female member, on the eve of the Day of Atonement, is a survival of the former substitution of animal sacrifices in the place of man, as the accompanying prayer indicates: "May this animal be my atonement and substitute. May it go to death and I to a long and peaceful life." Just as animal sacrifices had formerly taken the place of human sacrifices, so have the former in turn been displaced by prayers. The prophets and other sacred writers of Israel urged the substitution persistently.[9] A relapse in case of Jewish restoration of the Jewish cult into its former usage of sacrifices is therefore no more possible than a similar relapse from animal to human sacrifices was possible in former times. But a stationary stage in the Jewish cult in the future is likewise unthinkable. The Jewish religion will be regenerated along with the people.

Note IX

Colonization movements, as we well know, do not arise merely from mere enthusiasm for a certain idea, but arise primarily, through the definite demands of life. They originate mostly in small countries, where the struggle for existence is very hard and are directed toward such places where opportunities for making a living are abundant. Colonization, being a kind of mass-migration under the protection of the law, endeavors to seek for labor a better soil and more extensive rights. If the Jews, with the help of France, should originate a mass-migration of their oppressed brethren into the Orient, it will take place only because the Jewish colonists will find a better field for gaining a livelihood, and Jewish labor receive at least as much legal protection as it enjoys in the Occident. It is to be asked, therefore, whether these fundamental conditions necessary for a Jewish settlement in the Orient already exist there. At present, this is not the case. Nor can we speak as yet of a Jewish mass-migration to the Holy Land. But a great vista of possibilities will be opened in the Orient in the near future, by means of the civilization which once proceeded from there. As a result of the rapidly-spreading lines of communication, geographical distance, and with it the difference between Occidental civilization and Oriental barbarism, are quickly disappearing. Civilization which, during the greater part of the historical development of humanity proceeded from East to West, has begun, since the French Revolution, its backward march over the globe. Even in geographical relations there has entered a

[6] Cf. II Kings iii, 27, the story of the sacrifice by Mesha, the Moabite King, of his eldest son.—*Translator.*
[7] Procob. Bell. Goth. lib. II, Chap. *25.*
[8] Zohar, Part I, p. 60, section Noah.
[9] See, among other passages, Hosea vi, 6; xiv, 4; Micah vi, 6-8; Isaiah 1, 11; lxvi, 1.

transformation in the movement of life; the closed circular movement took the place of the centripetal movements toward progress on the one hand, and toward its opposite, degeneration, on the other. The geographical center of culture, which relapsed for centuries in a death-like rigidity, after it had given the world the light of the spirit which was first kindled there, will again be restored to life and influence. The French tricolor already flutters proudly in Egypt and Syria, and the appellation applied by the French poet to the Syrian expedition is no longer a mere poetical expression, but a prophetic utterance.

Napoleon the First, who had undertaken an expedition into Egypt and the Saint Simonists group, one of which is at present at the head of the Suez enterprise, have already recognized how important it is for France to civilize the Orient. The French wars in the Crimea and Italy were only preparations for the solution of the Oriental problem. This solution consists in the reconciliation of Occidental culture with that of the Oriental Semites who until now have formed a historical typical contrast to the Indo-Germans. Ernest Renan has clearly described this contrast, but he has also emphasized the fact that the Semites possess the ability to awaken once more from spiritual death into a new life in a much higher degree than the Indo-Germans.

After the work on the Suez Canal is completed the interests of world commerce will undoubtedly demand the establishment of depots and settlements along the road to India and China, settlements of such a character as will transform the neglected and anarchic state of the countries lying along this road into legal and cultivated States. This can occur only under the military protection of the European powers. Sagacious French diplomacy has always planned to annex the Orient to the precincts of culture. Undoubtedly, envy, which has caused the French to oppose the liberation of Italy, will also effect the French Oriental political policy with desires for conquest and domination. The French have learned, since their great Revolution, to overcome the dualism of the Material and Ideal in social life, as the work from which I have quoted indicates. The Material in that plan does not exclude the Ideal, and the latter is not a mere dream but has a Material basis. The one who appeals to a higher ideal is as little a hypocrite because he has also material interests at heart, as the one who sees in the earthly root of human affairs, the budding forces of the higher spirit is a dreamer.

It is well understood that we speak of a Jewish settlement in the Orient. We do not, however, mean to imply a total emigration of the Occidental Jews to Palestine. Even after the establishment of a Jewish State, the majority of the Jews who live at present in the civilized Occidental countries will undoubtedly remain where they are.

The Occidental Jews, who have only recently broken their way through to culture and have acquired an honorable civic position, will not abandon the valuable acquisition so quickly even if the restoration of Judæa were more than a pious desire. Such a sacrifice of a prize acquired with great effort is hardly to be expected even from patriotic Jews, let alone the majority of our "educated" parvenues, who have succeeded in breaking off all relations with the Jewish family and their unfortunate brethren, and who are proud of the fact that they have turned their back on the misery of their people. Yet this will not prevent the nobler natures among them from interesting themselves more deeply in the people whom they really do not know any more, and support it in its historical mission, when it will have the courage to reclaim its ancient fatherland in a natural, human way.

There has been a central unity among the Jews at all times, even among those who were scattered to the very confines of the earth. Jews have maintained a relation with the spiritual center wherever it was. No nation has ever felt as keenly the excitement going on in the spiritual nerve-center as have the Jews. Every spiritual sensation spread rapidly from the center to the extreme periphery of the national organism. The dispersion, even to the very ends of the world, had not hindered, even in antiquity, the scattered members of this remarkable people from participating in every national undertaking, from sharing the fortunes and misfortunes of fate. To-day, when distance is no more an obstacle to communication, it is of little consequence to a Jewish State whether more or less of the Jewish race dwells within or without its borders. Already during the existence of the old Jewish State, many Jews lived in foreign countries. The Jew-hater Haman could already at the time of the Second Temple utter the words which even to-day the enemies of the Jews constantly repeat: "There is a nation scattered abroad and dispersed among the people." However, there is hardly any civilized nation to-day, members of which are not found in foreign lands, either as foreigners or as naturalized citizens. As long as a Jewish State does not exist as a member of the civilized nations of the world, the Jews who live in exile must necessarily strive to obtain naturalization and "emancipation", though they by no means abandon the hope of the restoration of the Jewish State. The nations which are no more under the tutelage of their Mediæval Christian war lords do not for a moment hesitate to grant the Jews equal rights, to which they are justly entitled for their unexampled loyalty and fidelity to their nationality.

Note X

The Hebrew newspaper *Hamagid,* which appears in Lyck, East Prussia, prints, in its issue of the 26th of March, a report of a meeting held in Melbourne, Australia, in December, 1861, in which Christian as well as Jewish notables participated. The President, Lyons, opened the meeting and declared its purpose to be, "to enable the Jews to acquire land on Mount Zion, on which houses for the accommodation of Jewish pilgrims should be built, and that this may serve as the first step toward a Jewish settlement in Palestine." After him, a Jewish scholar spoke in Hebrew, an interpreter translating his speech into English. He spoke on the same subject as a Jewish patriot, and his address was enthusiastically received. Then a Christian minister addressed the audience on behalf of the restoration of the Jews. "To which nation," he exclaimed, "should the Holy Land fall as an inheritance? To Turkey? She is already in the grip of death and her days are numbered. To France? Russia and England will prevent it, just as Russia and France will object to the rule of England; and France will oppose a Russian occupation. No one should inherit it but the Jews, who will thus come into their own patrimony, the land which their ancestors had acquired with the assistance of God." Finally, the Dean of the Melbourne University declared that for years he had continually told his countrymen that it will not take long before the Jews regain possession of the land which belongs to them and which was promised to them. His joy will be great to live to see the first step toward the carrying out of his dream. And no matter how small the beginning may be, he was confident that it will finally lead to the great goal. Like the second redemption from exile, so must also the third be effected in a natural way, with the help of God, and it is the sacred duty of Christians to help the Jews in their endeavor. It was then decided to appoint a Committee for the purpose of soliciting contributions throughout Australia in order to acquire land for the Jews in the Holy Land.

Before this report was published in East Prussia, and could hardly have been generally known, there appeared the third part of the work of Rabbi Hirsh Kalischer—*Emunoh Yeshoroh*—"The Right Faith". The opinions of three great Jewish authorities, which preface it, support the view of R. Kalischer, who is in total agreement with the Dean of Melbourne University, that the return from the third exile must take place in a natural manner, under the protection of the European powers and with the help of our influential race-brethren who seem to have been providentially called to their high position. "The first thing to-day," says the author, "is to found a Company for Jewish colonization in Palestine, to acquire land and prepare it for settlement." "There is no greater service for the pious Jew to perform," adds our author, "than to rebuild the ruins of the Holy Land."

POSTSCRIPT

At the last moment, when these letters and notes had already left the press, my attention was called to Fichte's attack on the Jews, in the *Kreuzzeitung,* and to a similar attack which was published last year in Berlin, in a pamphlet, entitled, *The Jews and the German State.*

I wish it had been possible for me to have seen this Christian-German product before. But as it is too late for detailed analysis, I wish to remark that one glance at the book convinced me that this anonymous author, recently converted to the Kreuzzeitung's party, is only a "speculative" atheist and revolutionary, with whom the German public has certainly little sympathy.

Made in United States
Orlando, FL
18 March 2024

44922445R00065